WORDLY WISE
3000

Book **9**

Kenneth Hodkinson
Sandra Adams

Educators Publishing Service, Inc.
Cambridge and Toronto

Cover design by Hugh Price

May 2002 Printing

ISBN 0-8388-2439-0

Lesson 1

Word List

Study the definitions of the words below; then do the exercises for the lesson.

acolyte
a´ kə līt

n. A person who assists in some religious services by carrying out minor duties; one who attends or assists, a follower.
[The movie director's *acolytes* hung on his every word.]

bibulous
bi´ byə ləs

adj. **1.** Given to the consumption of alcoholic drinks.
[Health education classes provide information about the damage that can result from an excessively *bibulou*s lifestyle.]
2. Highly absorbent.
[The dentist ordered an ample supply of *bibulous* paper on which to place her instruments.]

coalesce
kō ə les´

v. To grow together; to unite to form a whole.
[Dissatisfied Republicans and Democrats *coalesced* behind the third-party candidate.]

covert
kō´ vʉrt

adj. Not openly acknowledged; secret.
[The intelligence operation was supposed to be *covert*, but sophisticated technology revealed it.]

declaim
di klām

v. To recite something in the style of a public speech; to speak in a loud, theatrical way.
["To be or not to be—," *declaimed* the actor, "that is the question."]

delineate
di li´ nē āt

v. **1.** To describe vividly and in detail.
[In *Pride and Prejudice*, Jane Austen's description of the Netherfield ball *delineates* the social practices of late eighteenth-century upper-class England.]
2. To draw an outline of; to represent by drawing.
[In her studio, the architect *delineated* her plan for the new wing of the building.]

demagogue
de´ mə gäg

n. A leader who seeks power by appealing to people's emotions and prejudices and by making false claims and promises.
[During the 1950's, Senator Joseph McCarthy was a *demagogue* who played on people's fear of communism.]
demagoguery *n.*

encomium
en kō´ mē əm

n. (plural: *encomiums* or *encomia*) An expression of warm and enthusiastic praise; a tribute.
[At a dinner in his honor, the philanthropist received *encomiums* for his generous financial gift to the cancer center.]

obdurate
äb´ də rət

adj. Resistant to persuasion; inflexible.
[Despite our pleadings, Maisie remained *obdurate* in her determination to hike the hazardous trail.]
2. Persistent in wrongdoing.
[The judge reasoned that the *obdurate* high schooler would benefit more from focused education than from prolonged incarceration.]
obduracy *n.*

prescience
pre´ shē ənt

n. Foresight; knowledge beforehand of events.
[The ancient Greeks consulted oracles because they believed them to have the power of *prescience*.]
prescient *adj.*

protagonist
prō ta´ gə nist

n. The chief character in a drama or story.
[The *protagonist* in Shakespearean tragedy is usually a person destroyed by a character flaw such as jealousy or excessive ambition.]

sedulous
se´ jə ləs

adj. Completed with careful perseverance; diligent.
[Through their *sedulous* efforts, workers in Project HOPE delivered medicine and supplies to doctors and patients in the disaster zone.]

trenchant
tren´ chənt

adj. Expressed with vigor and penetrating insight; keenly perceptive.
[The reviewer's *trenchant* criticism did not please the book's author.]

utopia
yoo tō´ pē ən

n. A place or state of perfect social and political conditions.
[The *utopia* promised by communism failed to materialize in Eastern Europe.]
utopian *adj.*

valedictory
va lə dik´ tə rē

n. A farewell address, especially one given at a graduation ceremony.
[The *valedictory* is usually given by a student who has achieved great distinction.]
adj. Of or relating to such a farewell address.
[General Lee's *valedictory* remarks to the Army of Virginia were tinged with sadness.]
valediction *n.*

1A Understanding Meanings

Read the sentences in each group below. If a sentence correctly uses the word in boldface, write C on the line of the corresponding number below the group. If a sentence is incorrect, rewrite it so that the vocabulary word in boldface is used correctly.

■   1. To **delineate** something is to describe it.
   2. A **bibulous** gathering is one at which alcohol is consumed to excess.
   3. A **utopia** is a false promise.
   4. An **obdurate** person is one who sticks stubbornly to a position.
   5. A **covert** act is one that is open for all to see.

   1. _____

   2. _____

   3. _____

   4. _____

   5. _____

■ 6. An **encomium** is an expression of displeasure.
7. An **acolyte** is anything that brings about change.
8. **Demagoguery** is appealing to people's prejudices in pursuit of power.
9. A **prescient** person is one who is able to foresee what might happen.
10. A **valedictory** is a farewell address.

6. _____

7. _____

8. _____

9. _____

10. _____

■ 11. A **sedulous** effort is one that is halfhearted.
12. A **protagonist** is a person who is quick to criticize.
13. To **declaim** something is to deny having anything to do with it.
14. A **trenchant** comment is one that is vigorously expressed.
15. To **coalesce** is to come together into a single body.

11. _____

12. _____

13. _____

14. _____

15. _____

1B Using Words

If the word (or a form of the word) in boldface fits a sentence in the group below, write the word in the blank space. If the word does not fit, leave the space empty.

1. **declaim**
   (a) Pam said she would _____ the reward because she did not really need the money.
   (b) Sultan loves to _____ his views on educational reform to anyone who will listen.
   (c) "I didn't quite catch what you said, so would you please _____ it?"

2. **obdurate**
   (a) In winter, heavy frosts make the soccer field too _____ to play on.
   (b) Kumiko begged her parents to change their mind, but they were _____ .
   (c) Pulling out weeds was such _____ work that we soon quit.

3. **valedictory**
   (a) This brief note was Professor Higgs's _____ to her colleagues.
   (b) It is customary for presidents to give a _____ speech upon leaving office.
   (c) The cast members presented a Miró print as a _____ to the director.

4. **bibulous**
   (a) No _____ drinks will be served to those who are under twenty-one.
   (b) The office holiday party is no longer the _____ affair it once was.
   (c) Some people believe that drinking one glass of wine a day can be a healthful rather than a dangerously _____ act.

5. **protagonist**
   (a) Macbeth is the _____ of Shakespeare's tragedy of that name.
   (b) England was France's _____ in the Hundred Years' War (1337-1453).
   (c) Every _____ in the 100-meter dash was given a chance of winning.

6. **coalesced**
   (a) The two automobiles _____ during the accident.
   (b) The political parties looked for a leader around whom they could _____ .
   (c) Water molecules begin to _____ when the temperature drops to 0 degrees centigrade.

7. **prescience**
   (a) Dario's decision to take the earlier train suggested _____ when he learned that the later train had derailed.
   (b) Farmers frequently show great _____ regarding the weather.
   (c) With the completed project due in two days, the designers felt a great amount of _____ .

8. **sedulous**
   (a) She gave a _____ grin when I discovered her prank.
   (b) The work in the midday sun is extremely _____, but you will be paid well for your efforts.
   (c) After the blizzard, the snow removal crews were _____ in their efforts to clear the streets.

1C Synonyms, Antonyms, Analogies

Each group of four words below contains two words that are either synonyms or antonyms. Circle these two words; then circle the S if they are synonyms, the A if they are antonyms.

1. VALEDICTION   PRAISE
   DEMAGOGUE   SALUTATION   S   A

2. SECRET   COVERT
   OBDURATE   SILENT   S   A

3. FLEXIBLE   PRESCIENT
   OBDURATE   HONEST   S   A

4. FOLLOWER   BULLY
   ACOLYTE   PROTAGONIST   S   A

5. UTOPIAN   ENORMOUS
   VAGUE   TRENCHANT   S   A

Complete the analogies by selecting the pair of words whose relationship most resembles the relationship of the pair in capital letters. Circle the letter in front of the pair you choose.

6. DECLAIM : VOICE ::
   (a) strike : bat   (c) hear : ear
   (b) drink : thirst   (d) gesture : hand

7. BIBULOUS : ALCOHOL ::
   (a) scrupulous : care   (c) ferocious : tiger
   (b) gluttonous : food   (d) gregarious : words

8. ENCOMIUM : PRAISE ::
   (a) agility : speed   (c) valedictory : farewell
   (b) mile : distance   (d) antidote : harm

9. SEDULOUS : DILIGENT ::
   (a) responsible : reliable   (c) priestly : religious
   (b) utopian : city   (d) trenchant : dull

10. COALESCE : SCATTER ::
    (a) converse : talk   (c) unite : divide
    (b) delineate : describe   (d) disclaim : proclaim

1D Images of Words

Circle the letter of each sentence that suggests the numbered boldface vocabulary word. In each group, you may circle more than one letter or none at all.

1. demagoguery
(a) The man claimed to be a doctor, but actually he knew little about medicine.
(b) The speaker argued that improving government-sponsored health-care benefits to older citizens would cost too much.
(c) Making subtle appeals to racial prejudice in order to get votes is shameful.

2. covert
(a) The overthrow of the Bokhari government took most people by surprise.
(b) Though they try to hide it, it's obvious that Terry and Marcel are in love.
(c) The agents were disappointed when their sting to catch the smugglers failed.

3. acolyte
(a) The tree was just four feet high when we planted it.
(b) Although the neurosurgeon performed the crucial procedures, the resident helped throughout the operation with the routine ones.
(c) The apprentice watched as the mason began constructing the curved wall.

4. delineate
(a) With a few quick pencil strokes, Roz captured Sean's bemused expression.
(b) Roberta repeated that she had been home since eight o'clock and knew nothing about the theft.
(c) Charles Dickens' ability to portray characters vividly is widely acknowledged.

5. encomium
(a) "They didn't give me enough time to do the job properly."
(b) "Be careful! Look where you're going!"
(c) This humidifier has received the highest ratings from an independent testing center.

6. valediction
(a) "Everything I am I owe to my angel mother" is one of Abraham Lincoln's better known quotes on his personal life.
(b) "A plague on both your houses!" cried Mercutio.
(c) "Pisa Pizza has the best calzones in town."

7. utopian

(a) My grandparents came to this country, seeking a new life.

(b) Our group is monitoring the water quality in the bay.

(c) One day, poverty and crime and disease will be banished from the earth.

8. protagonist

(a) David Ho, M.D., *Time* magazine's 1996 Man of the Year, works fastidiously in his fight to defeat the AIDS virus.

(b) Audrey Hepburn played the leading role in the Broadway musical *My Fair Lady*.

(c) Isaiah moved his queen and without looking up said, "Checkmate."

9. trenchant

(a) The soldiers positioned themselves in a way that prevented a surprise attack.

(b) Caroline did not think much of Stephen King's latest book.

(c) "The negotiator's comment cut right to the heart of the matter in the dispute between management and labor."

10. prescience

(a) "I think I'm going to be ill," Helen murmured.

(b) Harry felt certain the car would break down as soon as the warranty expired.

(c) The next full moon will be on the ninth of October.

1E Narrative

Read the narrative below; then complete the exercise that follows it.

INVISIBLE MAN

During the summer of 1945, Ralph Ellison lived on a friend's farm in Vermont, recuperating from a stress-related illness, a result of his wartime service in the Merchant Marine. He hoped to use the time to write. Even though he was little known as an author, he had written essays about literature for years. One day as he sat at his typewriter, he pecked out the words, "I am an invisible man."

At first, he was unsure what the sentence meant, but as he pondered it, a number of ideas relating to his identity as an African American began to **coalesce** for him. Although at the time he was unaware of the impact his book would have, he had begun writing one of the most significant novels of the twentieth century. It took him seven years. When the work was published in 1952 as *Invisible Man,* the **encomiums** that greeted it (including the National Book Award for fiction in 1953) ensured its instant status as a classic American novel. It has held this position ever since. One frequently mentioned feature of the book is the use Ellison makes of the richness and diversity of African-American speech and experience. Another feature often noted is the **prescience** of the book. Many of the events **delineated** in the novel have parallels in the civil rights and black power movements that erupted in the United States within a few years of its publication.

The **protagonist** of *Invisible Man* is an unnamed African American. He is invisible as an individual because white Americans, blinded by racial stereotypes, see only the color of his skin. The novel begins with his graduation from a high school in the South. He has been asked to give the **valedictory** address. Later he is invited to present his speech before a gathering of the town's leading white male citizens and to receive a scholarship from them. This turns out to be a **bibulous** occasion, at which the entertainment is a fight pitting Invisible Man and his classmates against each other. His speech is almost forgotten. Bruised and bloodied from the fight, Invisible Man **declaims** his speech; but still dazed from the melee, he uses the words "social equality" in place of "social responsibility." One of the men in the audience angrily challenges him, informing him: "We mean to do right by you, but you've got to know your place at all times." The rest of the novel concerns Invisible Man's attempts to "find his place," and it is emphatically not the place to which white America has consigned him.

Dropped from the college because he has unwittingly embarrassed the president of the school, Invisible Man travels north to New York to look for work. After a series of jobs, he becomes an **acolyte** of Brother Jack, the leader of the Brotherhood, a group that hopes to further their goals of social change by using the discontent of African Americans over discrimination. Modeled in part on the Communist Party, which sought a **covert** alliance with African Americans for its own political ends, the Brotherhood offers a **utopian** vision of equality. However, Invisible Man gradually understands that he and other black members are being used by the organization.

The **demagoguery** of Ras the Exhorter, leader of a black separatist group, offers as little hope for change to African Americans as the false promises of the Brotherhood do. In the midst of a violent riot, spawned in part by the Brotherhood and taken up by Ras and his followers, Invisible Man takes shelter inside an underground coal cellar from which vantage point he tells his story. In the closing passage of the novel, he announces, "I'm shaking off the old skin and I'll leave it here in the hole. I'm coming out, no less invisible without it, but coming out nevertheless. And I suppose it's damn well time."

In the years that followed, Ellison's **trenchant** critique of race relations in America was not well received by militant African-American leaders, who viewed him as an apologist for white America. But Ellison was **obdurate** in his insistence that literature was not propaganda for particular causes. In one of his essays he states, "I had to accept the fact that if I tried to adapt to their point of view, I would not only be dishonest but would violate disastrously that sense of complexity, historical and cultural, political and personal, out of which it is my fate and privilege to write."

For the next forty years, Ellison worked **sedulously** on a second novel. When he died in April 1994, it was still unfinished and consisted of some fifteen hundred manuscript pages kept in no particular order in several cardboard boxes. Ellison's widow invited his longtime friend John Callahan, a professor of literature, to shape this material into a novel. The resulting 368-page work, titled *Juneteenth*, was published in 1999 to mixed reviews. *Invisible Man* had set an extraordinarily high standard that the second book, in the view of some critics, failed to match. Ellison once said, "I would rather write one good book than five bad ones." In the end that is, perhaps, what he did.

Answer each of the following questions in a sentence. Whenever a vocabulary word does not appear in the question, try to use one (or a form of one) in your answer. In a few cases, both question and answer may contain vocabulary words.

1. Why would it be inaccurate to say that Ellison presents a **utopian** view of African–American life in *Invisible Man*?

   _____

2. Why is it unusual for a **protagonist** to have no name?

   _____

3. Why can we assume that the gathering of white citizens grew more raucous as the evening progressed?

   _____

4. What effect did the sentence "I am an invisible man" have on Ralph Ellison?

   _____

5. What kind of work do you think Invisible Man did for Brother Jack?

   _____

6. What details in the story suggest that Ras probably **declaimed** his ideas to those who would listen?

   _____

7. Why would the **prescience** of the ideas in the book not have been apparent on publication?

   _____

8. What details suggest that Invisible Man was **sedulous** in his studies?

   _____

9. How does the narrative indicate that Ellison's response to his critics was not **covert**?

   _____

10. How do you know that Invisible Man was **obdurate** in refusing to take the place that white society had assigned him?

_____

11. In what way was the reception of *Juneteenth* different from that of *Invisible Man*?

_____

WORDLY WISE

A **covert** act is one that is hidden or kept secret. The term comes from the French verb *couvrir,* "to cover." Its antonym is *overt.* An *overt* act is one that is open for all to see. This word comes from the French *ouvrir,* "to open."

Since *pro-* means "for," and *anti-* means "against," it would seem reasonable to assume that *antagonist* and **protagonist** are antonyms, but such is not the case. *Antagonist* derives from *anti-,* "against," and the Greek *agon,* "a struggle," and means "one who opposes or struggles against another." *Protagonist* is actually formed from *proto-,* "first," and the Greek *agonistes,* "an actor," and means "the main character in a play or story." In ancient Greek drama, the *protagonist* was the first actor to occupy the stage and engage in dialogue with the chorus.

Sir Thomas More was an English statesman and author. In 1516, he wrote *Utopia,* a description of an ideal state governed by reason. The title derives from the Greek *ou,* "not," and *topos,* "place." It literally means "no (such) place." The word entered the language unchanged as a noun and acquired an adjective form *utopian.* Unless naming the place described by More, the word is not capitalized.

Lesson 2

Word List

Study the definitions of the words below; then do the exercises for the lesson.

absolve
ab zälv´

v. To clear guilt, or to free from a promise or a responsibility.
[The court-ordered DNA test *absolved* the suspect of the assault charges.]

adumbrate
a´ dəm brāt

v. **1.** To foreshadow in an indirect way.
[The League of Nations *adumbrated* the United Nations.]
2. To outline in a sketchy way; to partially disclose.
[The architect Norman Foster *adumbrated* his idea for Bilbao's subway entrances, saving the details until later.]

apothegm
a´ pə them

n. A short, instructive saying.
[What do you think of the *apothegm* "Easy come; easy go"?]

aspersion
ə spʉr´ zhən

n. A defamatory expression; slander.
[Casting *aspersions* on another's good character is a despicable act.]

coadjutor
kō ə jo͞o´ tər

n. One who works with another, usually in a subordinate position; an assistant.
[The film director's *coadjutor* arranged the schedule so the production ran smoothly.]

congenital
kən je´ nə təl

adj. Existing at or dating from birth; being an essential characteristic.
[Surgeons can now make dramatic improvements on *congenital* physical abnormalities.]

élan
ā län´

n. A lively spirit with a distinctive style.
[The band played with such *élan* that it was invited to lead the parade.]

germane
jər mān´

adj. Pertinent and fitting.
[During her press conference, the governor refused to answer questions that weren't *germane* to her proposed budget.]

hiatus
hī ā´ təs

n. An interruption or gap in space, continuity, or time.
[The sculptor expressed frustration at the *hiatus* in his productivity in recent years.]

immure
i myo͞or´

v. To confine within or as if within walls; to imprison.
[Rapunzel let down her long hair to escape from the high tower in which she was *immured*.]

ineluctable
i ni lək´ tə bəl

adj. Not to be avoided or changed; inevitable.
[The *ineluctable* involvement of the United States in European affairs began in 1917.]

internecine
in tər ne´ sēn

adj. **1.** Marked by slaughter; mutually destructive.
[The *internecine* fighting among gangs distressed the community.]
2. Relating to conflict within a group.
[Word leaked to the outside world of the *internecine* struggle among Iraq's ruling elite.]

invoke in vōk´	*v.* **1.** To appeal to earnestly. [The petitioners *invoked* the support of their Congressional representatives to continue public television funding.] **2.** To cite in justification. [The witness refused to testify by *invoking* her Fifth Amendment right against self-incrimination.]
prototype prō´ tə tīp	*n.* A person or thing that serves as an example of its kind; an original. [The *prototype* of the automobile actually did look like a horseless carriage.]
quadrennial kwä dre´ nē əl	*adj.* **1.** Occurring every four years. [Presidential elections are a *quadrennial* event in the United States.] **2.** Lasting four years. [The governor's *quadrennial* term of office ends next January.]

2A Understanding Meanings

Read the sentences in each group below. If a sentence correctly uses the word in boldface, write C on the line of the corresponding number below the group. If a sentence is incorrect, rewrite it so that the vocabulary word in boldface is used correctly.

■ 1. A **hiatus** is a lapse in continuity.
   2. A **congenital** issue is one that both parties agree on.
   3. A person with a vigorous, assured manner might be said to have **élan.**
   4. **Aspersions** are unfavorable or damaging remarks.
   5. To **adumbrate** something is to give a broad sketch of it without details.

   1. _____

   2. _____

   3. _____

   4. _____

   5. _____

■ 6. An **apothegm** is a scientific theory.
   7. A **quadrennial** experiment is one that is of four years duration.
   8. To **immure** someone is to shut that person up in an institution.
   9. An **ineluctable** course is one that allows for slight variations.
   10. A **prototype** is a model upon which others are based.

   6. _____

   7. _____

8. _____

9. _____

10. _____

■ 11. A **coadjutor** is a fellow worker.
   12. To **absolve** someone is to reach a consensus with him or her.
   13. An **internecine** feud is one that involves conflict within a group.
   14. Something that is **germane** cannot be easily explained.
   15. To **invoke** a rule is to appeal to it in support of one's position.

11. _____

12. _____

13. _____

14. _____

15. _____

2B Using Words

If the word (or a form of the word) in boldface fits in a sentence in the group below it, write the word in the blank. If the word does not fit, leave the space empty.

1. **immured**
   (a) During the eighteenth century, prisoners in Paris were _____ in the fortress-like Bastille.
   (b) At first, the water dripping from the faucet was a terrible distraction, but then we became _____ to it.
   (c) Keeping the child _____ in the playpen keeps her from harm.

2. **prototype**
   (a) The _____ of the new engine is now ready for testing.
   (b) The ancient Greek city-state is the _____ of democratic institutions.
   (c) David Bushnell's 1775 underwater vessel was the _____ of submarines.

3. **élan**
   (a) The _____ of her earlier novels has been replaced by a deep melancholy.
   (b) The dancers from South America performed with such _____ they received a standing ovation.
   (c) The medium maintained he could communicate with a dead person's _____ .

4. **adumbrate**
   (a) Carlos took a few minutes to _____ his plan for rebuilding the business.
   (b) Those gathered before the painting _____ it in amazement.
   (c) Although an expert skier, Nastasia skidded on a patch of ice and _____ her right shoulder.

5. **invoke**
   (a) The court can _____ your license if you continue to get speeding tickets.
   (b) The hierarchy of the institution _____ a general assembly of its members.
   (c) The meeting opened with an _____ to a higher power.

6. **congenital**
   (a) The child's beautifully shaped hands are _____ characteristics evident even during infancy.
   (b) Nesim and Sadi are _____ twins who enjoy dressing exactly alike to surprise people.
   (c) The developing country's problems were _____ and, therefore, particularly challenging to its leaders.

7. **germane**
   (a) Your remarks, though interesting, are not _____ to this discussion.
   (b) It is _____ for a Scotsman to wear a kilt to a formal reception.
   (c) I made a _____ offer that the seller can either accept or reject.

8. **internecine**
   (a) His _____ ways aroused suspicion among his colleagues.
   (b) Yugoslavia's collapse led to _____ struggles among its former components.
   (c) Civil wars by their very nature are _____ affairs.

2C Synonyms, Antonyms, Analogies

Each group of four words below contains two words that are either synonyms or antonyms. Circle these two words; then circle the S if they are synonyms, the A if they are antonyms.

1. INHERENT   GERMANE
   CONGENITAL   DESTRUCTIVE   S   A

2. ASPERSION   HIATUS
   RESISTANCE   DEFAMATION   S   A

3. ATROCITY   INELUCTABLE
    DUBIOUS   INTERNECINE   S   A

4. IRRELEVANT   QUADRENNIAL
    REVEALING   GERMANE   S   A

5. ÉLAN   APOTHEGM
    MAXIM   MINIMUM   S   A

Complete the analogies by selecting the pair of words whose relationship most resembles the relationship of the pair in capital letters. Circle the letter in front of the pair you choose.

6. QUADRENNIAL : FOUR ::
   (a) triangular : three
   (b) annual : one
   (c) fifth : five
   (d) double : two

7. IMMURED: WALLS ::
   (a) delineated : lines
   (b) camped : tents
   (c) caged : bars
   (d) moored : dock

8. FORERUNNER : ADUMBRATE ::
   (a) resister : relieve
   (b) prospector : flourish
   (c) transformer : change
   (d) detriment : encourage

9. ABSOLVE : LIBERATE ::
   (a) adumbrate : delineate
   (b) immure : free
   (c) invoke : plead
   (d) forgive : forget

10. ACOLYTE : COADJUTOR
    (a) student : teacher
    (b) prototype : original
    (c) blunder : correction
    (d) demagogue : preacher

2D Images of Words

Circle the letter of each sentence that suggests the numbered boldface vocabulary word. In each group you may need to circle more than one letter or none at all.

1. **hiatus**
(a) The rope snapped because it wasn't strong enough to support the weight.
(b) We were so busy I had time for just a fifteen-minute lunch break.
(c) Freida resumed her studies after a year spent traveling in Australia.

2. absolve

(a) After deliberating for three hours, the jury returned a verdict of not guilty.
(b) It was clearly established that Marco was not responsible for the accident.
(c) I regret that I will not be able to attend Jacinda's retirement dinner.

3. invoke

(a) The press's opposition to censorship derives from the First Amendment.
(b) Why do you call him Robbie when you know he likes to be called Bob?
(c) After being wounded, the Cyclops prayed to his father Poseidon to doom Odysseus's trip home to Ithaca.

4. coadjutor

(a) Harry Hopkins served President Roosevelt in an unofficial capacity.
(b) The queen relied on her ladies-in-waiting to see that her wishes were carried out.
(c) The clerk for the chief justice prepared the brief for the case.

5. quadrennial

(a) An elm tree grew at each corner of the New England town's main square.
(b) The square root of 16 is 4.
(c) The governor of Alabama is elected for a four-year term.

6. aspersion

(a) "The people who live in this neighborhood cannot be trusted."
(b) "Alice has been in poor shape for some time."
(c) "The hurricane did extensive damage to the Florida panhandle."

7. adumbrate

(a) Sandra Day O'Connor has served on the Supreme Court since 1981.
(b) This newspaper article is about the trials of a family who face a major illness without health insurance.
(c) I had to read the passage in Virginia Woolf's *To the Lighthouse* three times before I understood its meaning.

8. ineluctable

(a) A person who carries this gene is predisposed to develop Alzheimer's disease.
(b) Water freezes at 32 degrees Fahrenheit.
(c) If you exercise and eat sensibly, you should increase your chance of living a long and healthy life.

9. internecine

(a) The meeting broke up without the members coming to an agreement.
(b) The secret ingredient in this mouthwash gives it a refreshing taste.
(c) The school's four houses were named Opal, Pearl, Agate and Ruby.

10. **apothegm**

(a) Into every life a little rain must fall.

(b) If you want to dance, you have to pay the fiddler.

(c) Be careful what you wish for because you might get it.

2E Narrative

Read the narrative below; then complete the exercise that follows it.

THE SPECIAL OLYMPICS

When John F. Kennedy was elected president in 1960, his entire family was thrust into the spotlight, with one exception. Since 1942, his younger sister Rosemary had been in an institution for the mentally retarded. The decision by the family to place her there had been painful but had been preceded by years of her increasingly disruptive behavior. At that time to be **immured** in an institution for life was the **ineluctable** fate of most victims of severe mental retardation. While it provided little for those who were locked up, for many of the families it gave the feeling that they were **absolved** of difficult obligations, and it spared them embarrassment and inconvenience. In many cases it also bore out the truth of the **apothegm** "Out of sight, out of mind."

Mental retardation is not mental illness. It manifests itself as impaired intellectual development and comes in many forms. There is a bewildering variety of causes, some **congenital**, others the result of brain injury, disease, or even a lack of emotional stimulation in early childhood. This general condition affects over seven million Americans, almost a quarter of them children. Ninety percent of these are classed as mildly retarded, meaning they score poorly on intelligence tests but are capable of functioning well from day to day in many other ways. Sadly, those with mental impairment are often the victims of **aspersions** made by thoughtless or unkind people. Excluded from group activities, denied the opportunity to shine, and assailed by doubts of their own self-worth, they understandably tend to withdraw from social contact.

All this began to change in the late 1960s. The indirect cause was Rosemary Kennedy, whose tragic fate inspired her younger sister, Eunice Kennedy Shriver, to initiate an athletic meeting for the mentally retarded. Shriver headed the Joseph P. Kennedy Jr. Foundation, which funded research on mental retardation. She **invoked** the help of Olympic gold medalist Rafer Johnson, a family friend who advised the Kennedy Foundation on fitness programs for the mentally retarded. After she had **adumbrated** her vision of a sports training program and competition, he agreed to work with her as **coadjutor**.

Their collaboration led to the first Special Olympics, held on July 20, 1968, at Soldiers Field, Chicago; this became the **prototype** for future Special Olympics. More than one thousand athletes who were mentally impaired in some way arrived from twenty-six states and Canada to compete in track-and-field events, floor hockey, and swimming. They did so with an **élan** that astonished family members and friends, who were there to cheer them on. No longer shunted off to the sidelines, they were now the center of attention and reveled in it. Not everyone won a medal, but no one felt like a loser. In addition, the competitors left the stadium knowing that special training programs were in place to help them do even better next time.

Over the next quarter century, Shriver and Johnson, together with an army of volunteers, saw the Special Olympics grow to become the largest amateur sports organization in the world, involving nearly a million mentally retarded children and adults. Local and state preliminary competitions lead up to the **quadrennial** Special Olympic World Games. The 1999 Special Olympic Summer World Games, held in Raleigh, North Carolina, drew over seven thousand athletes from more than one hundred countries.

Sports journalist Diana Nyad compared the event to the Olympic Games of ancient Greece when the **internecine** warfare among its city-states was put on hold for the month-long duration of the games. She added, "The mentally impaired athletes of the Special Olympics embrace their games as a **hiatus** from their constant war—the struggle to gain acceptance and respect in their everyday lives. Differences of color, religion, and politics are not **germane** to Special Olympians. They have a mission: to develop fitness, demonstrate courage, experience joy, and participate in the sharing of gifts, skills, and friendship with their families, other Special Olympic athletes, and the community."

Answer each of the following questions in a sentence. Whenever a vocabulary word does not appear in the question, try to use one (or a form of one) in your answer. In a few cases, both question and answer may contain vocabulary words.

1. What are some causes of mental retardation?

   _____

2. What are some problems mentally retarded people face?

   _____

3. In what way is life now different for people with mental retardation compared to the 1950s?

   _____

4. Why is the **apothegm** "nothing ventured, nothing gained" a good description of Eunice Kennedy Shriver's efforts in 1968?

   _____

5. How have the Olympics provided a **prototype** for the Special Olympics?

   _____

6. What was Rafer Johnson's role in the first Special Olympics?

   _____

7. Why would it be inaccurate today to say that people with mental retardation face an **ineluctable** fate?

   _____

8. How do you know that the athletes enjoyed participating in the first Special Olympics?

   _____

9. According to the narrative, what factors have been **germane** to the successful development of the Special Olympics?

   _____

10. Why do you think the Special Olympic World Games are held **quadrennially**?

    _____

11. According to Diana Nyad, in what way is the benefit of Special Olympics to people with mental retardation today similar to the benefit of the Olympics to the Greeks long ago?

    _____

WORDLY WISE

One of the meanings of **adumbrate** is "to foreshadow," and the word itself suggests this; it is formed from the Latin prefix *ad-*, "toward" and *umbra,* "shadow."

When something is in shadow, its details cannot be clearly seen, and this is suggested by the word's other meaning, "to give an outline of," since to do so is to explain without going into too much detail. A common word that shares this Latin root is *umbrella*; as well as keeping off the rain, it provides shade from the sun.

The Latin prefix *in-*, "in" or "inside," changes to *im-* before certain consonants for ease in pronunciation, as in *immure* where it combines with the Latin *murus*, "wall." To **immure** someone is to keep that person locked up inside a walled place of confinement. *Mural,* "a picture painted on a wall," comes from the same root.

A **quadrennial** event takes place every four years. The word is formed from the Latin *quad-* or *quadri-*, "four," and *ennium* from *annus,* "year." Related words are formed from *bi-,* "two"; *tri-,* "three"; *decem,* "ten"; and *centum,* "one hundred." A *biennial* event occurs every two years; a *triennial* event occurs every three years; a *dicennial* event occurs every ten years; and a *centennial* event occurs every hundred years.

Lesson 3

Word List

Study the definitions of the words below; then do the exercises for the lesson.

amalgam
ə mal´ gəm

n. **1.** An alloy of mercury and other metals.
[Silver *amalgam*, which was commonly used for filling teeth, is being replaced by a composite of other materials.]
2. A mixture of different elements.
[The report is a curious *amalgam* of practical proposals and questionable claims of past accomplishments.]

antediluvian
an ti də lo͞o´ vē ən

adj. Very old or old-fashioned.
[In this age of cell phones, faxes, and e-mail, picking up a pen to write a letter seems almost *antediluvian*.]

apothecary
ə pä´ thə ker ē

n. One who prepares and sells ointments, drugs, and similar items for medicinal purposes.
[Romeo convinced the impoverished *apothecary* to sell him the deadly poison illegally.]

ascetic
ə se´ tik

adj. Refraining from self-indulgence.
[Henry David Thoreau lived an *ascetic* life during his two years in a cabin at Walden Pond.]
n. A person who practices self-denial.
[As he searched for the meaning of life, the man who became the Buddha lived for many years as an *ascetic*.]

beneficent
bə ne´ fə sənt

adj. Doing or producing good.
[Quitting smoking has a *beneficent* effect on the health even of smokers of long duration.]

charlatan
shär´ lə tən

n. One who falsely claims knowledge or ability.
[Anyone whose program promises dramatic weight loss without the need to diet or exercise is a *charlatan*.]

denizen
de´ nə zən

n. An inhabitant, resident, or frequenter of a place.
[In several of his novels, Marcel Pagno vividly delineates the *denizens* of small rural towns of southern France.]

doyen
doi´ ən

n. **1.** A senior member of a group, especially one who is highly respected.
[Anthropologist Louis Leakey was the *doyen* of a small group searching for evidence of human origins.]
2. The oldest example of a category.
doyenne *n.* The female equivalent of *doyen*.

flora
flôr´ a

n. Plants considered as a group in a particular area or era.
[Prominent among the *flora* of Florida are dozens of varieties of palm trees.]

imbibe
im bīb´

v. **1.** To consume by drinking.
[As the designated driver, I will not *imbibe* even one alcoholic drink.]
2. To absorb or take in mentally.
[The graphic arts students *imbibed* the capabilities of the new computer with enthusiasm.]

nostrum näs´ trəm	*n.* A medicine or remedy whose effectiveness has not been proven. [Here is a *nostrum* that the makers claim reverses hair loss.]
obviate äb´ vē āt	*v.* To prevent or make unnecessary; to get rid of. [Frequent oil changes may *obviate* the need for expensive engine repairs.]
perennial pə re´ nē əl	*adj.* Lasting indefinitely or recurring. [Until they received financial counseling, incurring credit-card debt was a *perennial* problem for that family.] *n.* A plant that lives three or more years. [Her garden includes some of my favorite *perennials*—irises, poppies, and peonies.]
putative pyoo´ tə tiv	*adj.* Commonly accepted or supposed; assumed to exist. [Isabel Marlowe is the *putative* heir to the Goldstone fortune and will go to court to prove her claim.]
savant sa vänt´	*n.* A person with detailed knowledge in a specialized field. [Thomas Jefferson was a self-taught *savant* in several diverse areas of knowledge.]

3A Understanding Meanings

Read the sentences in each group below. If a sentence correctly uses the word in boldface, write C on the line of the corresponding number below the group. If a sentence is incorrect, rewrite it so that the vocabulary word in boldface is used correctly.

■   1. A **beneficent** substance is one that promotes health.
    2. A region's **flora** is all the flowers that grow in it.
    3. **Antediluvian** customs are those that take place in or on water.
    4. A **perennial** topic is one that keeps coming up again and again.
    5. An **amalgam** is a mixture.

1. _____

2. _____

3. _____

4. _____

5. _____

■   6. A **savant** is a clever or witty remark.
    7. A **denizen** of the ocean is a creature that lives there.
    8. An **ascetic** is a person who possesses a great deal of knowledge.
    9. To **imbibe** facts is to take them in.
   10. To **obviate** something is to go around it.

6. _____

7. _____

8. _____

9. _____

10. _____

■ 11. An **apothecary** is a person who sells medicinal preparations.
   12. The **doyen** of a group is the respected leader of it.
   13. A **nostrum** is an offensive remark.
   14. A **putative** claim is one that has yet to be proven.
   15. A **charlatan** is a person who falsely claims expertise.

11. _____

12. _____

13. _____

14. _____

15. _____

3B Using Words

If the word (or a form of the word) in boldface fits a sentence in the group below it, write the word in the blank space. If the word does not fit, leave the space empty.

1. **denizen**
   (a) The crocodile is a feared _____ of Africa's upper Nile.
   (b) The elderly _____ of the village seldom ventures out of doors in winter.
   (c) That word is a _____ of the dictionary and is seldom seen anywhere else .

2. **amalgam**
   (a) Most dentists now avoid filling teeth with _____ because of its mercury content.
   (b) Racial prejudice is an _____ of ignorance and fear.
   (c) The judge will decide whether the _____ of the two companies is legal.

3. **flora**
   (a) Cynthia arranged the _____ in a tall glass vase.
   (b) The Earth's _____ began over a billion years ago with simple algae.
   (c) The _____ of the Siberian tundra is mostly made up of mosses and lichens.

4. **perennial**
   (a) The delphinium is a _____ that comes back year after year.
   (b) With three young children, daily life in the house was marked by _____ activity.
   (c) Route One is a _____ highway that extends from Maine to Key West, Florida,

5. **ascetic**
   (a) These vitamins have an _____ effect on me.
   (b) The plush, blue velvet curtains enhanced the _____ quality of the room.
   (c) During the war, with many items rationed, most people had no choice but to practice an _____ lifestyle.

6. **obviate**
   (a) The new bridge will _____ the need to increase the ferry service.
   (b) Our friends tried to _____ us from leaving, but we insisted that we had to go.
   (c) A clear directive from the manager will _____ any confusion that may exist among employees .

7. **imbibe**
   (a) Plants _____ moisture through their roots.
   (b) Students in the humanities course _____ a knowledge of Latin and Greek classics.
   (c) The school can _____ no more than fifty students in its freshman class.

8. **doyen(ne)**
   (a) Skier Diana Golden, whose twenty-nine gold medals were won after multiple surgeries, has become the _____ of disabled athletes.
   (b) Camilla is running for the position of _____ of the senior class.
   (c) The giant redwood is the _____ of the plant kingdom.

3C Synonyms, Antonyms, Analogies

Each group of four words below contains two words that are either synonyms or antonyms. Circle these two words; then circle the S if they are synonyms, the A if they are antonyms.

| 1. | SAVANT | BENEFICIARY | | |
| | PHARMACIST | CHARLATAN | S | A |

| 2. | REALISTIC | DEADLY | | |
| | BENEFICENT | PUTATIVE | S | A |

3. ONGOING   GERMANE
   PERENNIAL   ASCETIC   S   A

4. IMBIBE   REQUIRE
   OBVIATE   ALTER   S   A

5. CONTEMPORARY   TRENCHANT
   ANTEDILUVIAN   OUTRAGEOUS   S   A

Complete the analogies by selecting the pair of words whose relationship most resembles the relationship of the pair in capital letters. Circle the letter of the pair you choose.

6. APOTHECARY : MEDICINE ::
   (a) parent : child   (c) demagogue : speech
   (b) baker : bread   (d) doctor : patient

7. MONK : ASCETIC ::
   (a) dog : germane   (c) priest : bibulous
   (b) savant : intelligent   (d) alien : familiar

8. FERN : FLORA ::
   (a) orchestra: music   (c) rhyme : poetry
   (b) novel : literature   (d) village : city

9. IMBIBE : LIQUID ::
   (a) cook : meat   (c) inhale : gas
   (b) boil : water   (d) develop : prototype

10. DOYEN : DOYENNE ::
    (a) hog : sow   (c) mouse : mice
    (b) father : son   (d) cow : calf

3D Images of Words

Circle the letter of each sentence that suggests the numbered boldface vocabulary word. In each group, you may circle more than one letter or none at all.

1. nostrum
(a) The Salk and Sabin vaccines have greatly reduced the incidence of polio.
(b) Eighty milligrams of aspirin is the dosage in this children's pill.
(c) Doctors once bled their patients in efforts to restore them to health.

2. ascetic
(a) For breakfast, Sadie has just a bowl of cereal and a glass of orange juice.
(b) Most plants thrive where there is rich soil, water, and sunshine.
(c) The costumes for the show were kept as simple as possible.

3. antediluvian
(a) Before the valley was flooded for the reservoir, this was rich farmland.
(b) I was surprised to see farmers still using horse-drawn plows.
(c) These air traffic controllers maintain that their computers are outdated.

4. perennial
(a) The mint that I planted five years ago has spread over much of the garden.
(b) Joe could never make his paycheck last until Friday and always tried to borrow from someone else on the job.
(c) The factory runs for 24 hours a day 365 days a year.

5. doyen(ne)
(a) Amelia Earhart was the most respected aviator of her time.
(d) Maria said the quality she most admires in another person is honesty.
(c) The marathon is one of the most demanding of all Olympic events.

6. savant
(a) I don't think Ms. Williams is aware of what is going on in her department.
(b) Marie and Pierre Curie discovered radium and studied the properties of this radioactive substance.
(c) They say that no one knows more about language than Noam Chomsky.

7. apothecary
(a) The sign above the door said "Medicines and Potions Sold Here."
(b) "Something to help you sleep?" the old woman said. "I have the very thing."
(c) The patient went from the operating theater to the recovery room.

8. charlatan
(a) Zambor sold Seth a metal bracelet guaranteed to cure his rheumatism.
(b) For one thousand dollars Rama will give you the secret of eternal youth.
(c) Randy shook his head and said there was nothing he could do to help me.

9. putative
(a) We assume that Khanda wrote the poem since it resembles her other work.
(b) I assumed the money was a gift since you said nothing about repayment.
(c) The detective assumed the identity of a petty thief to win the suspect's confidence.

10. beneficent
(a) Because of her asthma, my sister prefers the climate of Arizona.
(b) Fido's behavior improved after he attended dog obedience school.
(c) The Taj Mahal is one of the great architectural wonders of the world.

3E Narrative

Read the narrative below; then complete the exercise that follows it.

THE SECRETS OF THE FOREST

For most of human history, medicine was a curious **amalgam** of ancient dogmas, odd superstitions, and scientific truths, held together by blind faith in the **nostrums** dispensed by the practitioner. A patient could do little to differentiate the **charlatan** from the genuine healer; it was often a matter of luck whether the person who was ill recovered or got worse. Frequently, the best medical advice came from **apothecaries**, skilled herbalists, who derived their medicines and ointments from plants whose effectiveness had been proved by trial and error over the centuries.

The organic compounds called alkaloids, formed in the bark, roots, stems, leaves, or berries, give plants their healing properties. Their characteristic bitter taste can be an indication that a particular plant has useful medicinal properties, but alkaloids taken in large doses can also be deadly, causing sickness, paralysis, or even death. An extract called atropine, derived from the plant belladonna, a **perennial** of the nightshade family, can be **beneficent** or deadly, depending on how it is employed. Used properly it relieves muscle spasms; given in larger doses, it becomes a deadly poison.

In 1909, the *Journal of Pharmacology and Therapeutics* began publication in Baltimore, Maryland, an indication that scientists were studying the medicinal properties of plants in a more rigorous manner. At about the same time, researchers for pharmaceutical companies began developing synthetic alkaloids. The success of these products convinced many researchers that the future of drug research lay in the laboratory and not in nature, **obviating** the need to go tramping through field and forest on plant-gathering expeditions. Those who believed otherwise were regarded as **antediluvian** in their outlook. This attitude, however, changed several decades later when scientists discovered that new strains of organisms were resistant to synthetic drugs.

The science ethnobotany, the study of how the people of a particular region relate to the plants that grow there, came into its own when the limitations of synthetic drugs became obvious. The **doyen** of this discipline is Richard Schultes, a retired Harvard professor, who lived for extended periods among Native American people in North, Central, and South America. His research on mushrooms used by the Mazatec peoples of southern Mexico led to the development of Visken, a drug used to treat heart conditions.

When Schultes first visited the Amazon rain forest in the 1930s, the popular view of this remote part of the world, fed by jungle adventure stories and movies, was that its **denizens** were savages armed with blowguns and poison-tipped darts. Schultes disproved this notion, for he found the people he lived among to be gentle and peaceful. In particular, he learned a great deal from the tribal shamans, who functioned as both priests and herbalists. Many of them led **ascetic** lives in harmony with nature. Because of their role as healers in their communities, they had an encyclopedic knowledge of the medicinal properties of local **flora**, acquired from preceding generations and through experience. The eminent Harvard professor was happy to adopt the role of student, eager to learn from those whose knowledge in this area was clearly superior to his own.

Botanists who have studied the subject estimate that there are a quarter of a million plant species in the world. There could be as many as sixty thousand, many as yet unknown to Western science, in the Amazon rain forest. Sadly, this treasure house of nature is shrinking rapidly under the onslaught of logging operations that are creating new settlements and grazing lands for livestock. Plant species are disappearing at an alarming rate, and the **putative** loss to medical science is incalculable.

Not only plant species, but also the shamans who understand their healing powers are disappearing as Western popular culture penetrates the distant areas of the Amazon basin. To the young people, who eagerly **imbibe** this commercial culture of designer-labeled tee-shirts, transistor radios, canned soft drinks, and video games, the life of a shaman with its long apprenticeship, its harmony with the world of nature, and its simple lifestyle has little appeal. The ethnobotanists who go to the Amazon today are in a race against time as they seek to acquire knowledge before the last of these forest **savants** is gone. It is an odd fact that the shamans' apprentices today are college professors, many from the United States.

Answer each of the following questions in a sentence. Whenever a vocabulary word does not appear in the question, try to use one (or a form of one) in your answer. In a few cases, both question and answer may contain vocabulary words.

1. Will synthetic drugs be **obviated** by the research ethnobotanists are now conducting? Explain your answer.

   _____

2. Why is it likely that most of the medicinal plants the shamans use are **perennials**?

   _____

3. Why is the loss of medicinal plants in the Amazon rain forest described as **putative**?

   _____

4. What makes up the **flora** of the Amazon region?

   _____

5. What was Schultes's purpose in associating with the shamans?

   _____

6. Why would it be inaccurate to describe the shamans' encyclopedic knowledge of plants in their region as **antediluvian**?

   _____

7. In what way were the early **apothecaries** of the western world similar to the shamans of the Amazon region?

   _____

8. Hundreds of years ago, what were some of the problems a sick person faced when trying to get better?

   _____

9. Based on the details provided in the narrative about Schultes's career, do you think one could appropriately consider him a **doyen**? Explain your answer.

   _____

10. Why might alkaloids be described as "a double-edged sword"?

   _____

11. Why would it have been accurate to describe Schultes as a **denizen** of the Amazon region?

   _____

WORDLY WISE

The word **antediluvian** is formed from the Latin *ante-,* "before" and *diluvium,* "flood." The flood being referred to in this word is the one described in the Bible. According to the story, Noah built an ark to save himself and various pairs of animals from this deluge. Such an event would have to have occurred a very long time ago. Therefore, anything described as *antediluvian* would have to be extremely old.

There are two separate explanations for the origin of the word **charlatan**. The first is that it comes from the Italian *ciarlare,* "to chatter," a reference to the rapid talk of the seller that distracts customers while they are being deceived and separated from their money. The second is that it comes from *cerretano,* "a person from Cerreto," a town in Italy that was supposedly notorious for its smooth-talking vendors.

The term **flora** comes from Flora, the Roman goddess of flowers. The equivalent term for a region's animal life is *fauna,* derived from Faunus, a Roman god of nature whose followers were called fauns and were described as having the body of a man and the horns, ears, tails, and legs of a goat.

Lesson 4

Word List

Study the definitions of the words below; then do the exercises for the lesson.

approbation
a prə bā´ shən
n. An expression of approval; praise.
[The company's flexible-hours policy won the employees' *approbation*.]

benighted
bi nī´ təd
adj. Existing in a state of moral, cultural, or intellectual darkness; unenlightened.
[To insist that males and females perform only stereotypical, gender-based roles is *benighted*.]

bourgeois
boorzh´ wä
n. The middle class or a member of the middle class.
[Madame Loisel in Guy de Maupassant's "The Necklace" is miserable in her status as a member of the *bourgeois*.]

adj. Very concerned with middle-class values, such as respectability and material well being, with an inclination toward mediocrity.
[Was it really imperative to wear a suit to this event, Sam wondered, or was it just one more *bourgeois* demand for which he had no patience?
2. Reflecting mediocrity.
[Sam considered his neighbor's taste in home decorating to be *bourgeois*.]

credo
krē´ dō
n. A strongly held belief; a guide to one's action.
[The *credo* of the Three Musketeers was "All for one, and one for all."]

empirical
im pir´ i kəl
adj. Based on experience or observation as opposed to theory; capable of being confirmed by observation.
[Modern science began with insistence upon *empirical* data as opposed to unsubstantiated ideas of philosophers of the ancient world.]

eschew
e shoo´
v. To stay away from; to shun, especially on practical or moral grounds.
[Not a strict vegetarian, Rebekah *eschews* meat, although she will eat a few kinds of fish.]

expatiate
ek´ spa´ shē āt
v. To speak or write about in great detail; to elaborate, usually used with *on* or *upon*.
[The senator *expatiated* upon the need to preserve our dwindling wetlands.]

iconoclast
ī kä´ nə klast
n. One who attacks established beliefs, customs, or institutions.
[*Iconoclast* Betty Friedan rejected the notion that "biology is destiny" in her 1963 revolutionary work *The Feminine Mystique*.]
iconoclastic *adj.*

indigence
in´ di jənt
n. An extreme level of poverty.
[Many families reduced to *indigence* by the Great Depression of the 1930s traveled to California looking for work.]
indigent *n.* A person who is indigent.
adj. Without means of support.

laudable
lô´ də bəl
adj. Praiseworthy.
[The parents' efforts to save the publicly funded nursery school from being closed were *laudable* but marked by conflicts from the start.]

mandate man´ dāt	*n.* A clear command or instruction. [After years of battle with the French, in the 1960s the Muslim majority's vote in Algeria *mandated* its independence.] *v.* To require or order. [The Constitution *mandates* the right of an accused to a fair trial.]
ostensible ä sten´ sə bəl	*adj.* Only seemingly so; apparent. [His *ostensible* reason for stopping at the café was to socialize, but he was really trailing someone in his role as a private detective.]
recalcitrant ri kal´ sə trənt	*adj.* Unwilling to accept another's authority; stubbornly defiant. [In spite of Nicole's efforts to bring the *recalcitrant* horse into the trailer, it continued to pull back as soon as they reached the ramp.] **recalcitrance** *n.*
regurgitate rē gər´ jə tāt	*v.* **1.** To expel (partially digested food) from the stomach. [Some birds feed their young by *regurgitating* food into their offsprings' beaks.] **2.** To repeat mindlessly what one has learned. [Students need to develop critical thinking skills rather than merely *regurgitate* what they hear in a lecture.]
risible ri´zə bəl	*adj.* Provoking or causing laughter. [The actor declaimed King Lear's speeches in so pompous a manner that the effect was *risible* rather than moving.]

4A Understanding Meanings

Read the sentences in each group below. If a sentence correctly uses the word in boldface, write C on the line of the corresponding number below the group. If a sentence is incorrect, rewrite it so that the vocabulary word in boldface is used correctly.

■ 1. An **indigent** person is one who gets upset easily.
2. A **benighted** attitude is one that is lacking in common sense.
3. A **bourgeois** is a member of the upper class.
4. An **ostensible** purpose is one that only seems genuine.
5. A **laudable** objective is one that can be attained with little effort.

1. _____

2. _____

3. _____

4. _____

5. _____

■ 6. **Approbation** is a period during which a person's ability is evaluated.
7. **Empirical** evidence is that which is proved by actual observation.
8. An **iconoclast** is a leader, especially of a religious or church group.
9. A **risible** remark is one that provokes laughter.
10. **Recalcitrance** is stubborn defiance.

6. _____

7. _____

9. _____

9. _____

10. _____

■ 11. A **credo** is a personal belief or set of beliefs.
12. To **eschew** something is to think it over carefully.
13. To **mandate** something is to require it.
14. To **regurgitate** information is to repeat it when asked to do so.
15. To **expatiate** is to leave one's native country.

11. _____

12. _____

13. _____

14. _____

15. _____

4B Using Words

If the word (or a form of the word) in boldface fits in a sentence in the group below it, write the word in the blank space. If the word does not fit, leave the space empty.

1. eschew
   (a) Ballplayers would set a good example if they would _____ chewing tobacco.
   (b) I usually _____ Route 17 because the traffic on it is so heavy.
   (c) As part of my diet I _____ fried foods.

2. mandate
   (a) State governments have the right to _____ speed limits on our highways.
   (b) Queen Noor of Jordan is a _____ of that nation.
   (c) The baby-sitter's _____ stated that the parents would return by eleven.

3. **benighted**
   (a) The _____ philosophy of this school is that all children can learn, although they may do so in different ways.
   (b) When Winston was _____ by the queen, he became Sir Winston.
   (c) The Romanian leader's _____ rule was justly overthrown in 1988.

4. **regurgitate**
   (a) The baby will _____ milk if you let him gulp it too quickly.
   (b) Years ago, students were stuffed with facts that they _____ on their examinations.
   (c) The suspicious-acting stranger became quite _____ when I asked him what he was doing.

5. **empirical**
   (a) We employ the _____ method known as trial and error.
   (b) Geology is an _____ science that relies heavily on careful observation.
   (c) Rome went from a republican form of government to an _____ one in 27 B.C.

6. **bourgeois**
   (a) "You needn't be so _____ ," Ann said when Robert insisted on wearing a jacket and tie to dinner.
   (b) The stateswoman's manner is aristocratic rather than _____ .
   (c) Sidney's grades were _____ , but she hopes to do better next semester.

7. **ostensible**
   (a) The only _____ noise on that summer evening was the chirping of the crickets.
   (b) The _____ purpose of the visit is to see us, but there may be other reasons.
   (c) Papa can be so _____ when he digs in his heels that it's useless to argue.

8. **expatiate**
   (a) United States Representative Barbara Jordan eloquently _____ upon the reasons for impeachment of President Richard M. Nixon.
   (b) Mr. Drury _____ on his daughter's successes in a ten-page letter to me.
   (c) During the potato famine in their country, many of the Irish _____ , never to return.

4C Synonyms, Antonyms, Analogies

Each group of four words below contains two words that are either synonyms or antonyms. Circle these two words; then circle the S if they are synonyms, the A if they are antonyms.

1. APPROBATION   CRITICISM
   INDIGENCE   PRESCIENCE   S   A

2. OBDURATE   PERENNIAL
   RISIBLE   SOLEMN   S   A

3. BENIGHTED   DEFICIENT
   RECALCITRANT   PUTATIVE   S   A

4. MANDATE   ENCOMIUM
   BELIEF   CREDO   S   A

5. LAUDABLE   EMPIRICAL
   DESPICABLE   BIBULOUS   S   A

Complete the analogies by selecting the pair of words whose relationship most resembles the relationship of the pair in capital letters. Circle the letter in front of the pair you choose.

6. INDIGENT : MONEY ::
   (a) doctor : physician   (c) savant : knowledge
   (b) doyen : respect   (d) invalid : health

7. BOURGEOIS : CLASS ::
   (a) gap : hiatus   (c) protagonist : play
   (b) B+ : grade   (d) 1/4 : 0.25

8. ICONOCLAST : REVERENCE ::
   (a) savant : wealth   (c) apothegm : wisdom
   (b) soldier : élan   (d) charlatan: honesty

9. MANDATE : AUTHORIZATION ::
   (a) expatiate: confusion   (c) direct : instructions
   (b) cooperate : aspersion   (d) regurgitate : food

10. EXPATIATE : ADUMBRATE ::

    (a) imbibe : swallow   (c) coalesce : assuage

    (b) invoke : spurn   (d) obviate : predict

4D Images of Words

Circle the letter of each sentence that suggests the numbered boldface vocabulary word. In each group, you may circle more than one letter or none at all.

1. credo

(a) I believe that Amber had a baby boy.

(b) Sharon still believes in the tooth fairy.

(c) Claude Monet maintained that the real subject of his paintings was light.

2. iconoclast

(a) Rosie acts as if everyone else is stupid.

(b) Einstein changed forever the classical scientific view of space and time.

(c) The outspoken Irish writer George Bernard Shaw was also a critic and social reformer.

3. approbation

(a) "Their work does not seem good enough for this construction project."

(b) "Satisfaction guaranteed or your money back."

(c) "Well done!"

4. recalcitrance

(a) Neither partner would apologize to the other after the argument.

(b) The screw-top lid is so tight that I can't get it off.

(c) All our efforts to rid the lawn of dandelions have failed.

5. laudable

(a) Granny's hobby is taking care of stray cats and finding them homes.

(b) After doing poorly in school at first, Graham started getting A's and B's.

(c) The Hospice movement brings comfort to the terminally ill and their families.

6. risible

(a) After setting a goal of $10,000, fund organizers actually raised only approximately half that amount.

(b) Jay climbed onto the horse and found himself facing the wrong way.

(c) The smell of bacon reminded us that we had not yet had breakfast.

7. empirical

(a) Observers report greatly increased sightings of bald eagles.

(b) I know the paint isn't dry yet because I touched it to find out.

(c) Sunlight can be separated into all the colors of the rainbow.

8. **indigence**

(a) "I can't believe you thought I'd lie! " cried Yolande.

(b) The patient has no insurance and is unable to pay the hospital bill.

(c) The castaways despaired when the plane flew away without spotting them.

9. **ostensible**

(a) They often think of ways to show that they are rich.

(b) They claimed to be tourists, but the F.B.I. suspects them of spying.

(c) I usually drive into town, but today I decided to walk.

10. **mandate**

(a) There is no reason for you to do all the work yourself when I can help you.

(b) Julie ran ten miles a day while training for the marathon.

(c) Do you realize that a slice of chocolate cake with icing contains over four hundred calories?

4E Narrative

Read the narrative below; then complete the exercise that follows it.

HOUSE OF CHILDREN

Educational theory in the nineteenth century was based on the notion that students were empty vessels into which the teacher poured knowledge. Learners demonstrated their progress by **regurgitating** this information on tests; failing to do so was viewed as purposeful **recalcitrance** and punished accordingly. The idea that children have a natural thirst for knowledge and are capable of learning on their own if simply given the opportunity would have struck most pedagogues as **risible**.

Such was the climate of the time when Maria Montessori attended school. She was born in 1870 into a typical **bourgeois** Italian family—her father was a government finance official for the tobacco industry; her mother, an intelligent and articulate woman, ran the home. The schools Maria went to were no different from others attended by children of her social class; the girls and boys received instruction separately. Girls studied music, needlework, and household management, subjects appropriate for females who were taught to **eschew** any thoughts of professional careers and to prepare themselves to become dutiful wives and loving mothers.

While she was still in primary school, Maria's **iconoclastic** nature, which was to characterize her life, first became apparent. She expressed a desire to attend a technical school where she could study mathematics. Signor Montessori was shocked at the idea and refused to give his consent. Fortunately, Maria's mother supported her. Although, as a dutiful wife, she did not contradict her husband when he declaimed his ideas about a woman's role in society, Maria's mother eventually wore down his resistance. Maria attended the technical school and went on to study medicine at the

University of Rome, becoming the first woman in Italy to receive a medical degree. When she graduated in 1896, her father attended, smiling proudly. She had won his **approbation**. "I felt like a lion-tamer that day," she later recalled.

Psychiatry, the study of mental illness, was in its infancy at the turn of the century when Dr. Montessori chose it as her specialty. Children suffering from mental disorders were assumed to be unteachable and were kept locked in barren rooms with not one object to touch or hold. Appalled by this **benighted** attitude, Dr. Montessori set up a school for eight-year-olds in the institution to which she had been assigned. She taught classes based on **empirical** principles that she developed as she went along. Guiding the children rather than instructing them, she provided materials that stimulated their senses. Her diminutive charges learned responsibility by caring for plants and small animals; they learned to keep themselves and their classroom clean and tidy. They were encouraged but not required to complete structured tasks, which Montessori developed for them. They were free to move about and arrange the classroom furniture for their convenience rather than for the teacher's.

While others in the field viewed Dr. Montessori's experiments as **laudable**, they believed they were bound to fail. However, when her students passed exams on a level with children outside the institution, her colleagues realized that they had underestimated her ideas. Montessori began to question the quality of education for all children. She wrote later in *The Montessori Method* that she "became convinced that similar methods applied to normal children would develop or set free their personality in a marvelous and surprising way." Because of her success, Dr. Montessori was invited to set up a school for the children of **indigent** families in Rome's poorest district. When she opened the school on January 6, 1907, she called it Casa dei Bambini or Children's House. The techniques and materials used there became a model for many such schools, initially in Italy and then throughout the world.

In 1922 the Italian government gave Dr. Montessori a **mandate** to revise the methods in the nation's public schools. By then her fame had spread throughout the world; in books, articles, and lectures she **expatiated** upon the lessons she had learned from those she had been **ostensibly** teaching. She expressed her **credo** in these words from *The Child in the Family*: ". . . children are weak human beings who live among the strong; they are not understood, and their profound needs are unrecognized by adult society." She ended her book with a warning: "Until the adults consciously face their errors and correct them, they will find themselves in a forest of insoluble problems. And children, becoming in their turn adults, will be victims of the same error, which they will transmit from generation to generation."

Answer each of the following questions in a sentence. Whenever a vocabulary word does not appear in the question, try to use one (or a form of one) in your answer. In a few cases, both question and answer may contain vocabulary words.

1. How did Maria Montessori develop her theories of education?

   _____

2. In what way were Montessori's views about working with children with mental disorders **iconoclastic?**

   _____

3. During Dr. Montessori's childhood, what was the **ostensible** reason for sending boys and girls to different schools?

   _____

4. If girls today were asked to follow the course of study used in Montessori's time, how do you think they would respond?

   _____

5. How do you know that Maria Montessori's father eventually viewed her educational choices as **laudable?**

   _____

6. How might Signor Montessori have expressed his **credo?**

   _____

7. Why would it be inaccurate to describe the students of Casa dei Bambini as **bourgeois?**

   _____

8. In what way were Montessori's ideas about education different from those that dominated when she was growing up?

   _____

9. How did the Italian government express its **approbation** of Dr. Montessori?

   _____

WORDLY WISE

Bourgeois (pronounced boor-zhwa) is both a singular and a plural noun as well as an adjective. It comes unchanged in meaning and pronunciation from the French and derives from the French *bourg*, "a town." *Bourgeoisie* (pronounced boor-zhwa-zee) is a collective noun that refers to the middle class as a whole.

Iconoclast is formed from the Greek *eikon*, "image," and *klastes*, "breaker" or "destroyer." The original iconoclasts were eighth and ninth century Christians who felt that reli-

gious images were false idols that should be destroyed. Many priceless works of art were lost as a result. Today's iconoclasts are less violent in their behavior.

Laud comes from the Latin *laudare*, "to praise." In addition to **laudable**, the adjective *laudatory*, which means "expressing praise," is formed from this verb. A losing but good-natured candidate in an election might give a speech that is both *laudatory* (by praising his or her opponent) and *laudable* (because the loser shows no bitterness).

Crossword Puzzle

Solve the crossword puzzle below by studying the clues and filling in the answer boxes. Clues followed by a number are definitions of words in lessons 1 through 4. The number gives the word list in which the answer to the clue is taken.

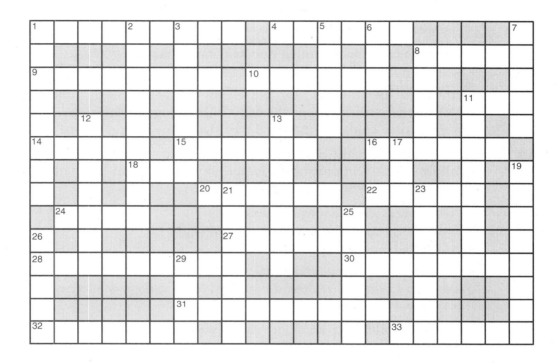

Clues Across

1. To speak or write about in great detail (4)
4. To stay away from; to shun (4)
8. The capital of Egypt
9. To come together to form one body (1)
10. Hidden from view; secret (1)
11. A falsehood
14. Of or from Ireland
15. To absorb or take in mentally (3)
16. An interruption in continuity or time (2)
18. "As easy as _____"
20. To appeal to earnestly (2)
22. The plants of a particular area (3)
24. Aid and _____
27. A person with much knowledge (3)
28. Showing foresight (1)
30. Poor or needy (4)
31. To outline in a sketchy way (2)
32. An inhabitant of a particular place(3)
33. Opposite of "after"

Clues Down

1. An expression of high praise (1)
2. Expressed with vigor and insight (1)
3. A person who practices self-denial (3)
5. A strongly held belief (4)
6. What you do when you are hungry
7. An eminent member of a group (3)
8. Large Asian country
11. Worthy of praise (4)
12. Provoking laughter; ridiculous (4)
13. To free from guilt or responsibility (2)
17. Not well
19. Commonly accepted or supposed (3)
21. A remedy of dubious value (3)
23. To prevent or make unnecessary (3)
25. Eight-foot clowns walk on these.
26. Driving with excessive _____ is dangerous.
29. A lively spirit with distinctive style (2)

Lesson 5

Word List

Study the definitions of the words below; then do the exercises for the lesson.

archaic
är kā´ ik
adj. Related or belonging to an earlier time.
[The wearing of wigs by British courtroom lawyers seems *archaic* to Americans.]

carouse
kə rouz´
v. To take part in noisy, often drunken, merrymaking.
[Some visitors to New Orleans during Mardi Gras *carouse* until the early hours of the morning.]

chicanery
shi kān´ rē
n. Clever deception through the use of misleading or confusing words or acts.
[Suspect some kind of *chicanery* if the offer seems too good to be true.]

contentious
kən ten´ shəs
adj. Causing or marked by argument or conflict.
[Politics is a *contentious* subject in our house because my step-father is a Democrat and my mom's a Republican.]

dissemble
di sem´ bəl
v. To conceal with an intent to deceive.
[When a witness clearly begins to *dissemble*, the jury can draw the appropriate conclusion.]

egregious
i grē´ jəs
adj. Conspicuously bad; flagrant.
[Although I believe that dissent is a right, I find *egregious* interruptions of a speaker unacceptable.]

execrate
ek´ sə krāt
v. To utterly abhor; to denounce as detestable.
[History can provide examples of countries once *execrated* as enemies who are later accepted as allies.]
execration *n.*

fealty
fē´ əl tē
n. Faithfulness; allegiance.
[The knights of the Round Table pledged *fealty* to King Arthur.]

microcosm
mī´ krə kä zəm
n. A small system that operates or develops like a larger system; a miniature world.
[College life is hardly a *microcosm* of the larger world.]

paroxysm
par´ ək si zəm
n. A sudden, violent, and uncontrollable action or occurrence.
[Although subject to frequent *paroxysms* of coughing, Laura obdurately denied it had anything to do with her smoking.]

pecuniary
pi kyōō´ nē er ē
adj. Having to do with money.
[The interests of the founders of the food co-op are more idealistic than *pecuniary*.]

rectitude
rek´ tə tōōd
n. High moral character.
[The umpire's faulty judgment is not a reflection of his *rectitude*.]

stratagem
stra´ tə jəm
n. A clever scheme for gaining an end.
[Lin's asking Tina to go to the movies was *a stratagem* to give us time to prepare for her surprise birthday party.]

stultify
stəl´ tə fī

v. To render useless or ineffectual; to weaken.
[Some policies in managed health-care systems *stultify* a physician's ability to provide timely, needed treatment for patients.]

vendetta
ven de´ tə

n. A blood feud; a prolonged and bitter feud.
[It took the deaths of Juliet and Romeo to end the *vendetta* between the Montagues and the Capulets.]

5A Understanding Meanings

Read the sentences in each group below. If a sentence correctly uses the word in boldface, write C on the line of the corresponding number below the group. If a sentence is incorrect, rewrite it so that the vocabulary word in boldface is used correctly.

■ 1. A **contentious** subject is one that arouses strong feelings and argument.
2. A **microcosm** is a measure of volume.
3. An **archaic** custom is one that seems out of place in the modern world.
4. A **stratagem** is a retreat from a previously held position.
5. To **execrate** someone is to shun that person.

1. _____
2. _____
3. _____
4. _____
5. _____

■ 6. **Chicanery** is the use of misleading words or acts in order to deceive.
7. A **vendetta** is a stall in a marketplace where inexpensive items are sold.
8. A **pecuniary** motive is one that involves financial gain.
9. **Fealty** is loyalty to a person, cause, or organization.
10. To **dissemble** is to fail to control one's emotions.

6. _____
7. _____
8. _____
9. _____
10. _____

■ 11. **Rectitude** is the demonstration of high moral stature.
   12. An **egregious** act is one that draws people together.
   13. To **carouse** is to ride round and round in circles.
   14. To **stultify** something is to render it ineffective.
   15. A **paroxysm** is a statement that appears to be contradictory.

11. _____

12. _____

13. _____

14. _____

15. _____

5B Using Words

If the word (or a form of the word) in boldface fits in a sentence in the group below it, write the word in the blank space. If the word does not fit, leave the space empty.

1. **egregious**
   (a) Robyn was not at all _____ and seemed to shun the company of others.
   (b) The bombing of the Oklahoma City Federal Building was an _____ crime.
   (c) An _____ error by the pilot almost caused the plane to crash.

2. **pecuniary**
   (a) She gave me a _____ look when I asked her what she had in her briefcase.
   (b) I worked as a _____ in my aunt's office until I started my own business.
   (c) An accountant is taking care of the _____ matters.

3. **contentious**
   (a) I was quite _____ to stay home, but Marsha wanted me to accompany her.
   (b) Baby Jessica becomes quite _____ if she misses her afternoon nap.
   (c) I took no further part in the discussion when it grew _____ .

4. **archaic**
   (a) Their speech was sprinkled with _____ expressions like "thee" and "thou."
   (b) Plowing with a team of oxen seems _____ to someone used to tractors.
   (c) The Lowells are a very _____ New England family.

5. **stultify**
   (a) When my cousin was young, she was told that smoking would _____ his growth.
   (b) Such a repressive school was bound to _____ her natural exuberance.
   (c) Absolute adherence to established procedures can _____ initiative within a company.

6. **microcosm**
   (a) Forty years ago, this town of fifty thousand inhabitants was a mere _____ of the community it was to become.
   (b) The fourteenth century castle was a _____ of medieval society.
   (c) A _____ is too small to be seen without a magnifying glass.

7. **stratagem**
   (a) A _____ looks like a rough pebble until it has been cut and polished.
   (b) In *The Iliad*, Homer describes how the Greek soldiers hid in the wooden horse as a _____ to gain entrance to Troy.
   (c) Moving her bishop was a _____ used by Bettina early in the chess game.

8. **paroxysm**
   (a) The actor threw himself to the floor in a _____ of uncontrolled grief.
   (b) When the clown performed for them, the children collapsed to the floor in a _____ of laughter.
   (c) "Truth is stranger than fiction" is a curious _____ .

5C Synonyms, Antonyms, Analogies

Each group of four words below contains two words that are either synonyms or antonyms. Circle these two words; then circle the S if they are synonyms, the A if they are antonyms.

1. ÉLAN   FEALTY
   PAROXYSM   LOYALTY   S   A

2. BLATANT   RICH
   PECUNIARY   EGREGIOUS   S   A

3. REVEL   EXECRATE
   CAROUSE   RESIST   S   A

4. PAROXYSM   CHICANERY
   RECTITUDE   TOLERANCE   S   A

5. ADVANCE   MICROCOSM
   MANEUVER   STRATAGEM   S   A

Complete the analogies by selecting the pair of words whose relationship most resembles the relationship of the pair in capital letters. Circle the letter in front of the pair you choose.

6. DESPISE: EXECRATE::
   (a) like : adore
   (b) hate : criticize
   (c) absolve : incriminate
   (d) declare : declaim

7. PECUNIARY : MONEY ::
   (a) perennial : plants
   (b) tropical : weather
   (c) military : armies
   (d) bourgeois : class

8. QUARREL : VENDETTA ::
   (a) apothegm: credo
   (b) gap : hiatus
   (c) pharmacist : apothecary
   (d) acolyte : leader

9. DISSEMBLE : DECEIVE ::
   (a) immure: emancipate
   (b) invoke: importune
   (c) debilitate: weaken
   (d) imbibe: feast

10. ARCHAIC : ANTEDILUVIAN ::
    (a) agrarian : urban
    (b) stratagem : plan
    (c) empirical : fictional
    (d) congenital : contagious

5D Images of Words

Circle the letter of each sentence that suggests the numbered boldface vocabulary word. In each group, you may circle more than one letter or none at all.

1. dissemble
(a) All you need to take the machine apart is a screwdriver and a wrench.
(b) The people left the meeting and went their separate ways.
(c) When I asked Monique about the sales figures for the day, I doubted her response.

2. vendetta
(a) No McCone would lift a finger to help a Madden, and vice versa.
(b) Garcia swore to have his revenge on the man who cheated his aunt.
(c) The Seminoles were forced from Florida onto reservations west of the Mississippi River.

3. rectitude
(a) Felicia has never had a day's illness in her life.
(b) The honesty of the Rodriguez family has never been called into question.
(c) The damage to the boat was slight and was easily repaired.

4. fealty

(a) The barons took a solemn oath to obey the king.

(b) The leader's acolytes did as he told them without question.

(c) When Hannah told her dog to shake hands, it raised its right front paw.

5. archaic

(a) Many laws that remain on the books are unenforced and all but forgotten.

(b) The house is a hundred years old but has been thoroughly modernized on the inside.

(c) It seems odd that a sword should still be part of an officer's dress uniform.

6. paroxysm

(a) The hurricane had attained speeds of 120 mph by late afternoon.

(b) The teenager collapsed and was taken away in an ambulance.

(c) It seems odd to speak of "a deafening silence."

7. carouse

(a) The earsplitting cries of the cats beneath my window kept me awake.

(b) Round and round and up and down went the brightly painted horses.

(c) The opera's opening scene is in a tavern courtyard filled with merrymakers.

8. execrate

(a) Marian Wright Edelman's anger at injustice led her to found the Children's Defense Fund in 1973.

(b) For the shame he had brought to his family, Li's name was never spoken.

(c) I attribute my activism to my dismay over living conditions in the old city.

9. microcosm

(a) The astronauts will live for several months at the space station.

(b) Jefferson's Monticello was a self-sufficient little world unto itself.

(c) A nuclear submarine can stay submerged for weeks at a time.

10. chicanery

(a) The practice of keeping pet monkeys is abhorrent to the veterinarian.

(b) Before they started, I paid the men half their fee for fixing my roof, and I never saw them again.

(c) I was suspicious when the caller promised to double my money in a month.

5E Narrative   *Read the narrative below; then complete the exercise that follows it.*

THE PALIO

The residents of Siena, a small, beautiful Tuscan city in the north-central region of Italy, continue to live and work along the stone streets and among the gothic buildings that remain almost unchanged since medieval times. In addition to maintaining their ancient architecture, they have also preserved a few **archaic** customs. One of these is a ninety-second horse race, the Palio, which has brought the city world renown. Since the 1600s on July 2 and August 16, it has been held in the city's main square, the Piazza del Campo. Ten jockeys riding bareback race their horses at breakneck speed three times around the square. The winner is the city district whose horse, with or without its rider, crosses the finish line first.

Siena comprises seventeen *contrade*, or districts, each with its own flag, animal emblem, church, museum, and social center. The rivalry among these districts, which goes back centuries, is given expression during the preparation and running of the Palio. The organization of the race, arising from years of tradition, is complex and includes many elements of chance.

Because of the narrowness of the track, only ten districts can compete: the seven excluded from the previous race plus three others, chosen by lot. The horses for the race are selected from local owners. After trial races are completed, each of the competing districts is allocated a horse, also determined by lot. The riders, who are professionals from outside Siena, have no **fealty** to any particular district. Motivated simply by **pecuniary** considerations, they hire themselves out to the highest bidder.

Each contrada has a particular enemy that it **execrates** above all others. Next to gaining possession of the coveted winner's banner, each district desires nothing more than the defeat of its historic rival. The responsibility for ensuring either of these outcomes falls to the district captains. While the **rectitude** of these neighborhood leaders is well known, they are permitted, in the days before the race, to set aside their scruples and engage in any form of **chicanery** to make certain that their contrada wins. They spread false rumors about the condition of their own or their competitors' horses, offer bribes to other riders, and temporarily eschew centuries-old **vendettas** to arrange secret deals with other districts not to obstruct each other during the race.

For the jockeys there is just one rule: they cannot interfere with each other's reins. Anything else is acceptable. During the race the riders deliberately bump into each other and block each other's mounts; they also strike other riders with their whips and try to throw them off balance by pulling at their clothing. These **egregious** acts, which in any other race would bring disqualification, not only go unpunished in the Palio, but are actually encouraged.

Around five o'clock in the afternoon of the race day, members of each contrada march through the city streets to the square. The spectators crowd the balconies of buildings surrounding the Campo or squeeze into the center of the square, enclosed by rails. Mattresses cover the walls of dangerous curves to protect both horses and riders.

Just before the race is to begin, nine of the horses with jockeys are clustered at the starting point. The tenth horse starts the race by charging the group from behind. The anticipation that has been building for days reaches a **paroxysm** of excitement as the horses and riders make their three wild circuits. The conclusion of the race brings great joy to the winning contrada and several days of carousing to most of Siena's residents.

The Palio may seem chaotic, bizarre, and violent to an outsider, but to the Sienese it makes perfect sense. In medieval times, Siena was a city-state surrounded by hostile neighbors. In order to maintain the peace or to achieve victory when war became inevitable, civic leaders resorted to carefully calculated **stratagems** to negotiate secretly with potential allies. They **dissembled** in order to throw their adversaries off guard and offered bribes where necessary. The Palio enacted in **microcosm** the realities of this larger world and provided a perfect opportunity to practice these unsavory but indispensable skills.

One result of the Palio has been the strong feeling of neighborhood unity created by the contrade through the preparations for the race and, at other times of the year, through the social activities and services provided to their residents. The Palio is also credited with reducing crime by offering an acceptable outlet for expressing angry and violent feelings.

In recent years, threats to the Palio's existence have come in varying forms. Animal rights advocates have raised the **contentious** issue of cruelty to the horses. Other observers have expressed fear that the urban sprawl beyond Siena's city walls could have a **stultifying** effect on the city's seventeen historic districts. And yet the Palio seems likely to continue. As one former mayor said, "The Palio helps Siena to survive in its own mind. It is a metaphor for the continuity of the life of the people."

Answer each of the following questions in a sentence. Whenever a vocabulary word does not appear in the question, try to use one (or a form of one) in your answer. In a few cases, both question and answer may contain vocabulary words.

1. Why is the Palio marked by so much **contention?**

    _____

2. Why would it be inaccurate to say that the primary motivation for winning the Palio is **pecuniary?**

    _____

3. In what way is the behavior of the contrada captains inconsistent?

    _____

4. Why is the Palio described as an **archaic** custom?

    _____

5. In what ways is the Palio a **microcosm** of an earlier period of Sienese history?

    _____

6. What details in the narrative tell you that contrade do not carry on **vendettas** against each other throughout the year?

    _____

7. How might the traditional rival of the winning contrada feel after the race?

    _____

8. In your opinion, what is the most **egregious** action a jockey could take during the race?

    _____

9. Which Sienese are unlikely to be **carousing** when the Palio is finished?

    _____

WORDLY WISE

At closing time in German beer halls, the call *Gar aus,* "All out!" was meant to indicate that it was time for everyone to leave. In fact, it became a signal for a last-minute drinking spree. The phrase entered English in the sixteenth century as **carouse,** and its meaning has remained unchanged to the present.

❖ ❖ ❖ ❖ ❖ ❖

The Latin *greg,* meaning "herd" or "flock," forms the root of several English words. *Gregarious* people like to be with others, rather like sheep staying close to the rest of the flock. To *congregate* is to come together, again in the manner of livestock drawn together. **Egregious** originally meant "sur-passing the rest of the flock" and was a term of approbation. Later, perhaps because it was used ironically, *egregious* acquired its present pejorative meaning.

❖ ❖ ❖ ❖ ❖ ❖

To **execrate** someone is to express extreme abhorrence of that person. Its original meaning was even stronger; it meant to put a curse on that person. This is clear from the etymology of the term. It comes from the Latin *ex-,* "away from," and *sacer,* "sacred." When you execrated someone, you stripped away what was sacred and left that person defenseless against evil forces.

Lesson 6

Word List

Study the definitions of the words below; then do the exercises for the lesson.

actuate
ak´ chə wāt

v. **1.** To cause to put into mechanical motion.
[A thermostat is *actuated* by changes of temperature.]
2. To cause to take action.
[Telecasts of the grievances of Native-American women *actuated* Wilma Olaya, a Cherokee, to return to Oklahoma where she became the tribe's first woman chief.]

brackish
bra´ kish

adj. **1.** Made up of a mixture of fresh water and seawater; salty water.
[Crabs thrive in the *brackish* waters of the estuary.]
2. Having an unpleasant taste.
[The coffee had been brewed hours before and was now so *brackish* that it was undrinkable.]

cognitive
käg´ nə tiv

adj. Relating to mental processes such as awareness, remembering, and reasoning.
[Failure to recognize and validate distinct *cognitive* learning styles can lead to the misdiagnosis of dysfunction.]

dissertation
di sər tā´ shən

n. A lengthy, usually written discussion of a topic, often for a college or university degree.
[On completion of her *dissertation* on phosphoarginine functions in invertebrates, Perry received her M.S. degree.]

dolorous
dō´ lə rəs

adj. Causing or marked by pain, misery, or sorrow.
[Mexican artist Frida Kahlo used graphic imagery to express grief in her *dolorous* self-portraits.]

endemic
en de´ mik

adj. Widespread or peculiar to a certain place or among a certain people.
[Malaria is *endemic* to the tropics.]

fecund
fe´ kənd

adj. **1.** Producing or capable of producing many offspring.
[Johann Sebastian Bach and his wife Anna were a *fecund* couple who had twenty children.]
2. Intellectually or artistically productive; creative.
[Bach was a *fecund* composer, and among his many works are some 300 sacred cantatas.]

genealogy
jē nē ä´ lə je

n. The history of a family and how its members are related to one another; also the study of such family histories.
[Martha can trace her family's *genealogy* all the way back to pilgrims on the *Mayflower* in 1620.]

inebriated
i nē´ brē ā təd

adj. Deprived of good sense and judgment, especially as the result of imbibing alcohol.
[SADD (Students Against Drunk Driving) make clear the horrors resulting from *inebriated* persons at the wheel.]

insidious
in si´ dē əs

adj. **1.** Seemingly harmless while actually being dangerous; treacherous or deceptive.
[The rogue's pose of rectitude was an *insidious* attempt to win our trust.]

2. Spreading harmfully in a subtle or gradual way.
[Watching too much television has an *insidious* effect on the minds of young children.]

interloper
in tər lō´ pər

n. One who intrudes on or interferes in the affairs of others.
[The tribe considered the tourists *interlopers* and resented their stares.]

precursor
pri kər´ sər

n. A person or thing that comes before and indicates the approach of another; a forerunner.
[Aching muscles can be the *precursor* of a bout of the flu.]

presentiment
pri zen´ tə mənt

n. A feeling that something is about to occur.
[An astute reader of Shirley Jackson's "The Lottery" will detect *presentiment* in the phrase, "Lottery in June; Corn be ready soon."]

ramification
ra mə fə kā´ shən

n. An outgrowth of a simple idea or plan; a resulting development or consequence.
[Eliminating the position of Department Chair has *ramifications* for all students in social studies courses.]

torpor
tôr´ pər

n. A state of mental or physical sluggishness or inactivity.
[Extreme heat often induces *torpor* in those unused to the tropics.]
torpid *adj.*

6A Understanding Meanings

Read the sentences in each group below. If the sentence correctly uses the word in boldface, write C on the line of the corresponding number below the group. If a sentence is incorrect, rewrite it so that the vocabulary word in boldface is used correctly.

■ 1. **Cognitive** faculties are those having to with mental functioning.
2. A **presentiment** is a cordial feeling one person has for another.
3. An **inebriated** person is one who is or seems to be intoxicated.
4. **Genealogy** is the study of rocks and fossils.
5. A **brackish** substance is one that is bitter to the taste.

1. _____

2. _____

3. _____

4. _____

5. _____

■   6. A **dissertation** is an act of abandonment.
    7. A **fecund** mind is one that comes up with many ideas.
    8. A **dolorous** occasion is one that is gloomy.
    9. A **precursor** is a sign of what is to come.
   10. A **ramification** is a means of forceful entry.

   6. _____

   7. _____

   8. _____

   9. _____

  10. _____

■ 11. An **insidious** illness is one that spreads without being noticed.
   12. A **torpid** person is one who is slow to respond.
   13. An **interloper** is a person who doesn't belong.
   14. An **endemic** problem is one that is specific to a particular area.
   15. To **actuate** a program is to move it beyond the planning stage.

  11. _____

  12. _____

  13. _____

  14. _____

  15. _____

6B Using Words

If the word (or a form of the word) in boldface fits in a sentence in the group below it, write the word in the blank space. If the word does not fit, leave the space empty.

1. **presentiment**
   (a) When the car broke down in thick fog, we were in a terrible _____ .
   (b) Your _____ that your luck was about to change turned out to be correct.
   (c) I asked the author to write a short _____ on the flyleaf of the book.

2. **fecund**
   (a) The _____ codfish lays thousands of eggs at a time.
   (b) Her _____ mind had the answer to every problem that presented itself.
   (c) Lope de Vega was the _____ author of nearly two thousand plays.

3. **cognitive**
   (a) The frontal lobes of the brain are equipped to deal with _____ tasks.
   (b) Dolphins and whales have _____ abilities different from those of humans.
   (c) He was in a _____ mood, so we were careful not to disturb him.

4. **insidious**
   (a) Roger was an _____ dresser and spent a small fortune on clothes.
   (b) The woman on the Dublin street appeared harmless but actually was an _____ informer for the enemy in Ireland's civil war.
   (c) AIDS is an _____ disease that may not reveal itself for many years.

5. **brackish**
   (a) After the hurricane, the _____ taste of the water made it undrinkable.
   (b) Its slow current causes the river to become _____ as it nears the sea.
   (c) The damp climate turns metal fittings _____ unless they are kept painted.

6. **torpid**
   (a) Cold-blooded creatures become _____ as the temperature drops.
   (b) I felt quite _____ at being unable to answer such an easy question.
   (c) The room grew _____ , and we were grateful for the extra blankets.

7. **inebriated**
   (a) Alex declined a glass of wine, fearing it would make him _____ .
   (b) The ink had been smudged, making the writing quite _____ .
   (c) A campaigner can become _____ with the sound of his own voice.

8. **endemic**
   (a) Joellen was admitted to the hospital when her bronchitis became _____ .
   (b) Violence has been _____ in the Balkans for centuries.
   (c) The patient's condition grew _____ , and doctors moved her to the intensive care unit.

6C Synonyms, Antonyms, Analogies

Each group of four words below contains two words that are either synonyms or antonyms. Circle these two words; then circle the S if they are synonyms, the A if they are antonyms.

1. CONSEQUENCE   MANDATE
   PRESENTIMENT   RAMIFICATION   S   A

2. LUCID   PRODUCTIVE
   INEBRIATED   INSIDIOUS   S   A

3. COGNITIVE   FECUND
   ENTICING   BARREN   S   A

4. INTERLOPER   FORERUNNER
   DEMAGOGUE   PRECURSOR   S   A

5. DOLOROUS   ASTUTE
   JOVIAL   BRACKISH   S   A

Complete the analogies by selecting the pair of words whose relationship most resembles the relationship of the pair in capital letters. Circle the letter in front of the pair you choose.

6. COGNITIVE : MIND ::
   (a) wise : savant   (c) empirical : doubt
   (b) verbal : speech   (d) ineluctible : change

7. INTERLOPER : RESENT ::
   (a) nostrum : cure   (c) denizen : inhabit
   (b) liquid : imbibe   (d) stratagem : dislike

8. ESSAY : DISSERTATION ::
   (a) pen : typewriter   (c) tune : song
   (b) student : teacher   (d) sketch : drawing

9. TEAR : BRACKISH ::
   (a) miser : frugal   (c) criminal : recalcitrant
   (b) disease : endemic   (d) seltzer : carbonated

10. BOREDOM : TORPOR ::
    (a) dislike : abhorrence
    (b) humor : hilarity
    (c) fan : devotee
    (d) delight : delirium

6D Images of Words

Circle the letter of each sentence that suggests the numbered boldface vocabulary word. In each group, you may circle more than one letter or none at all.

1. brackish

(a) The mud came up to our ankles as we trudged across the yard.
(b) The instruments were out of tune, and the sound grated on our ears.
(c) The undergrowth was so thick we could barely hack our way through it.

2. torpor

(a) In the midst of the heat wave, the elderly man could barely raise his head off the pillow.
(b) The rock ended up next to the gate after rolling down the hill.
(c) Regina stared vacantly ahead as though she had not heard my question.

3. insidious

(a) I didn't like country music at first, but it grew on me after I visited Nashville.
(b) If lead enters the blood its harmful effects may not show for years.
(c) The book on parenting advised against comparing one sibling with another.

4. actuate

(a) You cannot start the engine until you turn the key in the ignition.
(b) The leaves of the Venus's-flytrap snap shut when an insect lands on them.
(c) It's cynical to believe that people usually act in accord with what is in their own best interest.

5. fecund

(a) The dog barked so much that the neighbors could not get any sleep.
(b) Within three years of joining the company, Ricardo owned half of it.
(c) The village was quite small, but there were children everywhere.

6. precursor

(a) Putting the clock back an hour is a reminder that winter is almost upon us.
(b) Remember that *i* usually comes before *e* except after *c*.
(c) Within minutes of the sudden wind change, the storm began to rage.

7. dissertation

(a) The road ahead was closed, so we went into town by way of Hollyburn.
(b) Greta's paper on the Paris Commune was over two hundred pages long.
(c) Each speaker was given ten minutes, which left a little time for questions.

8. **interloper**

(a) Jonah was viewed with suspicion, for strangers were rare in those parts.

(b) Abdul moved with long, easy strides and won the race comfortably.

(c) Those brightly colored beads don't go with the rest of your outfit.

9. **ramification**

(a) If tuition is increased, many students may have to drop out of this college.

(b) Environmentalists protest the destruction of so many of these trees.

(c) All this trouble resulted from my leaving the car keys in the ignition.

10. **genealogy**

(a) Mary's great-great-grandfather was a cousin of George Washington Carver.

(b) These half-billion-year-old rocks were laid down during the Cambrian age.

(c) This registry lists births, marriages, and deaths since around 1800.

6E Narrative

Read the narrative below; then complete the exercise that follows it.

THE PATIENT'S DILEMMA

When Nancy Wexler received an unexpected call from her father in 1968 asking her to fly to Los Angeles to meet him, she had a **presentiment** that something was wrong. Her fears were justified. He had not wanted to tell her over the telephone that her mother was suffering from Huntington's disease, an illness first identified by Dr. George Huntington in 1872. The **dolorous** news came as a triple blow. Her mother would be subjected to devastating mental and physical deterioration before death mercifully ended her suffering. Then, since each child of a person afflicted with the disease has a fifty percent chance of inheriting the Huntington's gene, she and her older sister might endure a similar fate. Finally, should it turn out that either of them possessed the gene that brings on Huntington's disease, any children they might have would be at risk as well.

Huntington's disease (HD), which afflicts about thirty thousand people in the United States, is one of the cruelest and most **insidious** known to medical science because it affects the physical, mental, and emotional qualities of a person. Generally, the faulty gene does not become active until the person carrying it reaches early middle age; it is then that the symptoms first begin to appear. A stumble, a clumsy movement, or a memory lapse could be **precursors** of the onset of HD for a person at risk or could simply be trifling events that everyone experiences. Typically, the head and limbs of someone in an advanced state of the disease are jerked about, in the words of one observer, "as though manipulated by an **inebriated** puppeteer." Memory and other **cognitive** skills are also affected, resulting in personality changes and severe mental illness. The disease then progresses inexorably until death occurs around ten to twenty-five years after the disease begins. In 1968, there was no way of knowing beforehand if one would develop HD, because no test existed for the disease. Nor was there a cure.

In Wexler's doctoral **dissertation** to qualify as a clinical psychologist, she explored the **ramifications** of being one of the 150,000 people in the United States at risk for HD. She knew that many potential victims were overwhelmed by a feeling of futility when considering any meaningful plans for the future, and, as a consequence, often sank into a kind of **torpor**. But Wexler's response was to fight the disease. Along with her father, she began an intense lobbying and fund-raising effort. Their goal was to provide money for research to locate the HD gene, the first step in a possible cure.

In 1979, the year after her mother died, Wexler made the first of many trips to Lake Maracaibo in Venezuela. She had read some research related to a small, isolated community along the shores of this **brackish** lake; HD was **endemic** there. At first, the residents looked upon Wexler as an **interloper** and were alarmed by her presence, especially when she wanted to draw blood from them. Over time, however, she won their confidence. Her painstaking research indicated that the members of the community had a common female ancestor, who had lived around 1800. Wexler was fortunate that the preceding generations had been **fecund**. This allowed her to trace thirteen thousand descendents over ten generations. By analyzing the blood samples taken from all living members of the community, three hundred of whom had HD, Wexler, along with many other researchers who had joined the project, compiled the community's **genealogy**. This provided much of the evidence that scientists needed to locate the gene and develop a test to identify people who carried it.

In 1983, researchers created a highly accurate test for a genetic marker for HD; ten years later, the defective gene itself was located. Scientists discovered that the DNA molecules forming the gene repeat themselves in an abnormal manner. This "stutter" **actuates** the production of a protein that selectively destroys two small areas of the brain that control muscle movement. It is this toxic protein that causes Huntington's disease.

From her research, Wexler concluded that thirty percent of those at risk would decline to take a test to see whether they had the disease. However, a decade after the test became available, statistics revealed that the true figure was over eighty-five percent! Apparently, for many people at risk for HD, uncertainty is preferable to the possibility of learning the daunting fact that one has the disease. For this reason, genetic counseling has become a requirement for anyone who is to be tested. Professional counselors provide information and support both before and after the testing. Wexler herself declines to say whether she has been tested.

Answer each of the following questions in a sentence. Whenever a vocabulary word does not appear in the question, try to use one (or a form of one) in your answer. In a few cases, both question and answer may contain vocabulary words.

1. Why would a person with Huntington's disease in his or her family be alarmed if he or she stumbled or forgot something?

   _____

2. What role did Nancy Wexler play in **actuating** the research that enabled scientists to locate the gene for Huntington's disease?

   _____

3. Why is the discovery of the gene for Huntington's disease so important?

   _____

4. Why is Wexler considered an expert on the social consequences of Huntington's disease?

   _____

5. What suggests that Lake Maracaibo might be connected to the sea?

   _____

6. Why is **genealogy** so important in determining Huntington's disease?

   _____

7. Why would it be inaccurate to say that the people at Lake Maracaibo welcomed Wexler enthusiastically when she first arrived?

   _____

8. Why do you think genetic counseling is required for all who take the test to determine if they carry the gene for Huntington's disease?

   _____

9. Give two reasons why Huntington's disease is **endemic** in the Lake Maracaibo region.

   _____

10. What **ramifications** might the development of the test that identifies the HD gene have upon those at risk for the disease?

    _____

WORDLY WISE

Actuate and *activate* both relate to activity and both are derived from the Latin word *actus*, "act," but they have quite different meanings. *Actuate* means "to cause to put into action," while *activate* means "to make active." A person might be actuated by a desire for freshly baked bread to actually make some; the yeast added to the flour and water is what activates the dough, causing it to rise.

That which is **endemic** is particular to an area. That which is *epidemic* is spreading rapidly through infection in an area in which it is not usually prevalent. That which is *pan-demic* is so widespread as to be almost universal. All three words are derived from the Greek root *demos*, "people."

Interloper is a curious hybrid of a word, joining a Latin prefix, *inter-*, "between," to an old Dutch word, *lopen*, "to run." It was coined in the sixteenth century when English companies were given the sole right to trade with countries of the Far East. Foreign traders interfering with this right were called *interlopers*. The word soon lost this specialized meaning, and over the next hundred years it acquired its more general meaning of today.

Lesson 7

Word List

Study the definitions of the words below; then do the exercises for the lesson.

abjure
ab jŏor´

v. To renounce formally.
[Galileo was forced by the Catholic Church to *abjure* his belief that the earth circled the sun.]

amorphous
ə môr´ fəs

adj. Without a definite shape, boundary, or character.
[The amoeba's lack of a fixed structure gives it an *amorphous* shape.]

animus
a´ nə məs

n. 1. An attitude or spirit within a person that strongly influences him or her.
[A thoughtful reader will feel the *animus* that motivated Charlotte Brontë to write *Villette*.]
2. Deep-seated ill will.
[The *animus* between Serbs and Bosnians erupted into internecine war in the 1990s.]

dichotomy
dī kä´ tə me

n. Division into two distinct parts or groups.
[She argues that moral relativism blurs the *dichotomy* between good and evil.]

exemplar
ig zem´ plär

n. An example or model, especially an ideal one.
[Mahatma Gandhi was the *exemplar* of nonviolent resistance to injustice.]
exemplary *adj.*

herculean
hʉr kyə lē´ ən

adj. Of extraordinary size, power, or difficulty.
[Plowing the city streets after the blizzard of 1996 was a *herculean* task.]

inchoate
in kō´ ət

adj. Not fully formed or realized.
[Writers of fiction often explain that their *inchoate* ideas take shape as they write their novels.]

invidious
in vi´ dē əs

adj. Likely to cause resentment or animosity.
[The labor leader recited *invidious* facts about the company's lack of benefits for its employees.]

mélange
mā länzh´

n. A mixture of dissimilar materials.
[The garage sale was a *mélange* of clothes, furniture, and household bric-a-brac.]

nefarious
ni far´ ē əs

adj. Very wicked.
[The *nefarious* practice of enforced child labor is rampant in many poor countries.]

nihilism
nī´ ə li zem

n. A viewpoint that denies any meaning or value to life.
[His cynicism was so extreme that it bordered on *nihilism*.]
nihilistic *adj.*

ratify
ra´ tə fī

v. To approve, confirm, or verify.
[In a citywide referendum, voters *ratified* the ban on smoking in restaurants.]

subsume
səb sōōm´

v. To encompass in a larger or more comprehensive group; to include.
[In 1939, the work of other nuclear physicists was *subsumed* under the theory of fission proposed by Lise Meitner and Otto Frisch.]

variegated ver´ ē ə gā təd	*adj.* Varied as to form, type, or color. [The *variegated* leaves had stripes of green and white.]
vitiate vi´ shē āt	*v.* To impair or weaken. [Questionable sincerity *vitiated* her appeal for another chance.]

7A Understanding Meanings

Read the sentences in each group below. If a sentence correctly uses the word in boldface, write C on the line of the corresponding number below the group. If a sentence is incorrect, rewrite it so that the vocabulary word in boldface is used correctly.

■ 1. A **nefarious** scheme is one that is detestable.
2. To **vitiate** something is to give it renewed life or appeal.
3. An **exemplary** student is one who serves as a good example to others.
4. **Nihilism** is a doctrine that holds all life to be senseless and meaningless.
5. An **amorphous** object is one that is of great size.

1. _____
2. _____
3. _____
4. _____
5. _____

■ 6. **Animus** is a strong dislike or hatred.
7. A **dichotomy** is a split into two distinct parts.
8. A **variegated** surface is one that feels rough to the touch.
9. **Inchoate** hostility is animosity without a clear focus.
10. To **subsume** a division is to incorporate it into a larger one.

6. _____
7. _____
8. _____
9. _____
10. _____

■ 11. An **invidious** report is one that causes resentment.
 12. A **mélange** is a brawl.
 13. To **ratify** something is to formally repudiate it.
 14. To **abjure** a decision is to express approval of it.
 15. A **herculean** struggle is one requiring enormous effort.

11. _____

12. _____

13. _____

14. _____

15. _____

7B Using Words

If the word (or a form of the word) in boldface fits in a sentence in the group below it, write the word in the blank space. If the word does not fit, leave the space empty.

1. **amorphous**
   (a) From these _____ lumps of clay the potter produces objects of beauty.
   (b) _____ clouds of black smoke rose from the burning building.
   (c) Try to develop these _____ ideas into an organized narrative.

2. **exemplar**
   (a) The legendary Lancelot could not be celebrated as an _____ of knightly virtue.
   (b) Chartres cathedral in France is a fine _____ of Gothic architecture.
   (c) Her _____ teamwork earned her the praise of her coworkers.

3. **vitiate**
   (a) Tabloid television shows _____ the good taste of the viewing audience.
   (b) A number of glaring errors _____ the prosecution's case.
   (c) The medicine can be _____ by diluting it with water.

4. **nefarious**
   (a) The firefighters of Manhattan were heroic in their response to the _____ act intended to blow up the World Trade Center.
   (b) The river slowly wound its _____ way to the sea.
   (c) The _____ gangster Al Capone was convicted of income tax evasion.

5. **abjure**

   (a) During the peace talks, negotiators strove to convince Arab and Israeli leaders to _____ violence in settling their differences.

   (b) The company would have more credibility were it to _____ the absurd claims for the latest of its products.

   (c) The magician was able to _____ all kinds of objects out of thin air.

6. **mélange**

   (a) The _____ broke out when the two rival gangs met at the drive-in.

   (b) The vendor offered a _____ of used paperbacks and kitchen utensils.

   (c) The concert was a curious _____ of Dixieland jazz and chamber music.

7. **subsumed**

   (a) The old laws of physics were not discarded, but were _____ into the new.

   (b) Wales and Scotland were _____ into what became the United Kingdom.

   (c) If you _____ that I would like your plan, you are absolutely right.

8. **inchoate**

   (a) The solar system slowly formed itself from _____ interstellar matter.

   (b) In some mysterious way, the _____ pupa turns into the gorgeous butterfly.

   (c) The goal of advertising is to give shape and form to consumers' _____ longings.

7C Synonyms, Antonyms, Analogies

Each group of four words below contains two words that are either synonyms or antonyms. Circle these two words; then circle the S if they are synonyms, the A if they are antonyms.

1. DICHOTOMY   HOSTILITY
   SATISFACTION   ANIMUS   S   A

2. DIVERSE   HERCULEAN
   VARIEGATED   FRUSTRATED   S   A

3. STANDARD   EXEMPLAR
   MÉLANGE   DISPLAY   S   A

4. RATIFY   EXCLUDE
   DEPOSIT   SUBSUME   S   A

5. NIHILISTIC   OPTIMISTIC
   DESTRUCTIVE   NEFARIOUS   S   A

Complete the analogies by selecting the pair of words whose relationship most resembles the relationship of the pair in capital letters. Circle the letter in front of the pair you choose.

6. STRONG : HERCULEAN ::
   (a) actual : ostensible
   (b) bad : egregious
   (c) clear : brackish
   (d) relevant : germane

7. INVIDIOUS : RESENTMENT ::
   (a) archaic : appreciation
   (b) beneficent : scorn
   (c) risible : laughter
   (d) empirical : data

8. ABJURE : RATIFY ::
   (a) invoke : beseech
   (b) declare : declaim
   (c) shun : eschew
   (d) absolve : incriminate

9. AMOEBA : AMORPHOUS ::
   (a) gasoline : combustible
   (b) cost : exorbitant
   (c) gene : recessive
   (d) soldier : militant

10. VITIATE : FORTIFY ::
    (a) coalesce : consolidate
    (b) homogenize : diversify
    (c) debilitate : solidify
    (d) perpetrate : ameliorate

7D Images of Words

Circle the letter of each sentence that suggests the numbered boldface vocabulary word. In each group, you may need to circle more than one letter or none at all.

1. animus
(a) The painting is the work of an artist whose name is unknown.
(b) I don't know why she doubts me; I've always been forthright with her.
(c) The children were shy at first, but then they became quite lively.

2. herculean
(a) Organizations such as OXFAM America work to help people all over the world who face starvation.
(b) According to the Bible story, Samson used his great strength to pull down the temple of the Philistines.
(c) Rebuilding the towns hit by the earthquake will take many months.

3. variegated

(a) Looking down from the plane, we could see a patchwork of fields below.

(b) We tried several different approaches before we worked out a plan.

(c) The cat's fur was a curious mixture of black, brown, white, and gray.

4. amorphous

(a) Viewers gave various interpretations of the painting's brightly colored shapes.

(b) The diagram consisted of a triangle inside a circle inside a square.

(c) Neon lights created gentle images in the large puddles as the rain hit the city streets.

5. dichotomy

(a) She loved to wear her black satin shirt with her old blue jeans.

(b) In literature, the good Dr. Jekyll and the evil Mr. Hyde were one and the same person.

(c) The equator divides the world into its northern and southern hemispheres.

6. ratify

(a) Treaties with foreign powers must be approved by the Senate.

(b) The new student was reluctant to report the cheater.

(c) Despite its supporters' vigorous work and substantial gains, the Equal Rights Amendment has yet to become part of the United States Constitution.

7. mélange

(a) Any vegetables, chicken, and rice left over from yesterday were put into a pot with broth, cooked, and then served up for today's lunch.

(b) Her deep sadness moved everyone with whom she came in contact.

(c) The lemon pie was topped with a many-peaked mixture of whipped cream and sugar.

8. inchoate

(a) "I am working on an idea; I just can't adequately express it yet."

(b) From incoherent grunts and cries, somehow language emerged.

(c) Computation begins with simple addition and subtraction.

9. nihilism

(a) When asked what he believed in, Gospodin replied, "Nothing."

(b) If you start with 17 and take away 9 + 8, you are left with 0.

(c) Stalin ruled by terrifying the Russian people.

10. invidious

(a) For a while yesterday, bandits closed the border into Laos.

(b) The number 13 can be divided only by itself and 1.

(c) Pejorative terms applied to any group of people reflect the ignorance of the speaker.

7E Narrative

Read the narrative below; then complete the exercise that follows it.

CONSERVATION, STRUGGLE, AND INVENTION

The metaphor of America as a melting pot in which diverse cultural differences are **subsumed** into a single national identity has been replaced by that of a **variegated** mosaic, comprising numerous ethnic groups loyal to America but still strongly allied with the past that connects them to their native lands. The fastest growing group is the Hispanic Americans, the majority of whom are Chicanos who trace their roots back to Mexico. They live mostly in the Southwest and occupy a unique place among the country's ethnic groups, for as Chicano playwright Luis Valdez puts it: "We did not come to the United States at all. The United States came to us."

Valdez is referring to the Treaty of Guadalupe Hidalgo, **ratified** by Congress in 1848, which ended the war between Mexico and the United States. By its terms, the provinces lost to Mexico became the American Southwest and their inhabitants, citizens of the United States. But were they American or Mexican? After more than 150 years, during which time the Chicanos saw their Mexican heritage become **vitiated** by the dominant Anglo (non–Hispanic European culture), this **dichotomy** is still unresolved.

One area at issue is language. Most Chicano writers are bilingual, but do they express themselves in Spanish or English? Many choose a **mélange** of both, as in the following lines by Sandra Cisneros. Even in a tender love poem, she expresses an **animus** toward English: "Make love to me in Spanish. / Not with that other tongue. / I want you *juntito a mi* / Tender like the language crooned to babies."

Cisneros is one of an **amorphous** group of Chicano writers whose work reflects concern for economic, social, and political justice. Their **exemplar** is poet and author Tomas Rivera (1935–84). The son of migrant workers, he became a high school English teacher and later rose to become chancellor of the University of California. He recalls the **invidious** treatment of Chicanos by Anglo teachers: "we were whipped . . . for speaking Spanish on school grounds." In one of his articles, he lays out before his fellow writers and intellectuals the **herculean** task of *"conservación, lucha, e invención"*—to conserve the best of the past; to struggle for better economic, social, educational, and political conditions; and to invent a Chicano culture.

For the more politically active writers, the struggle to improve the conditions of migrant workers, many of them Chicanos like themselves, is a major concern. Prizewinning poet and teacher Gary Soto worked alongside migrants in the fields, and many of his poems reflect this experience: "After a day in the grape field near Rolinda / A fine silt, washed by sweat, / Has settled into the lines / On my wrists and palms. / Already I am becoming the valley. A soil that sprouts nothing / For any of us."

Another area of concern is the plight of the poorly educated urban Chicanos with bleak employment prospects, many of whom are drawn into **nefarious** street gangs. Their **nihilistic** attitude to life is captured in Luis J. Rodriguez's award-winning memoir *Always Running: La Vida Loca, Gang Days in L. A.* in which he captures the widespread despair through a young Chicano's reply to the police: "Go ahead and kill us. We're already dead."

Rodriguez, a poet and former gang member from East Los Angeles, understands the **inchoate** rage of gang members and tries to channel it into less violent forms. He founded Tia Chucha Press, which offers an opportunity for young Chicano writers to see their work in print. He writes, "I make sure to carry the tools of my trade. / Words and ideas. The kind that no one can take away. / So there may not be any work today, / But when there is, I'll be ready. / I got my tools."

All writers strive for success, but Chicano writers who achieve it face a difficult dilemma. Benjamin Alire Saenz, an English professor and former priest, understands this well. His novel *Carry Me Like Water* was sought after by fourteen New York publishers. It became a bestseller, was translated into several languages, and was sold to a movie studio. Inevitably thereafter, he felt the pressure to "broaden his appeal," to "write for a wider audience." But writers who **abjure** their cultural heritage and become identified as American rather than as Chicano authors, poets, or playwrights risk losing the identity that fueled their passion in the first place. On the other hand, those who stay close to their roots and write in Spanish or who deal exclusively with Chicano themes and concerns may not be whipped for their efforts, but neither will they achieve the national or even international recognition that all writers yearn for.

Answer each of the following questions in a sentence. Whenever a vocabulary word does not appear in the question, try to use one (or a form of one) in your answer. In a few cases, both question and answer may contain vocabulary words.

1. In what language do many bilingual Chicano poets express themselves?

_____

2. How do you know that poets and writers like Sandra Cisneros, Gary Soto, and Luis J. Rodriquez have not **abjured** their heritage?

_____

3. Why might a mosaic be a better metaphor for America than a melting pot?

_____

4. What is the **dichotomy** that many Chicanos experience in American society?

_____

5. Why would it be inaccurate to describe Tomas Rivera's ideas as **nihilistic**?

_____

6. How have many young poor, urban Chicanos expressed their **animus** toward society?

_____

7. How was Tomas Rivera an **exemplar** for Chicano writers?

_____

8. What are the long-term effects on a culture of such practices as the one described by Rivera?

_____

9. Why might Chicanos regard the Treaty of Guadalupe Hidalgo as **invidious**?

_____

10. What was Luis J. Rodriguez's purpose in setting up Tia Chucha Press?

_____

11. How did the Southwest become part of the United States?

_____

WORDLY WISE

The adjective **herculean** is sometimes capitalized, an indication that it is derived from someone's name. In this case, the character is Hercules, the hero of ancient Greek mythology who was called upon to perform twelve mighty labors to atone for murdering his wife and children. To be fair to Hercules, it should be mentioned that he committed this crime after Hera, the queen of the gods, had driven him insane. Any task requiring superhuman strength or power may be described as herculean or Herculean.

Nihilism comes from the Latin *nihil*, meaning "nothing," and the word has a number of applications, all of which are based on the idea of nothingness. At one extreme it is a philosophical concept that nothing is real, and the material world we think we inhabit is an illusion. In nineteenth-century Russia, nihilism became a political rallying cry, and the Nihilists believed that all government should be abolished and replaced with communal autonomy. In modern usage, it has a psychological meaning; it suggests an attitude devoid of morality, goodness, decency, and other such virtues.

Lesson 8

Word List

Study the definitions of the words below; then do the exercises for the lesson.

aborigine
abə rij´ ne

n. An original inhabitant, especially one displaced by later settlers.
[Mäori, *aborigine*s of New Zealand, comprise many tribes and subtribes.]
aboriginal *adj.*

abrogate
a´ brə gāt

v. To put an end to; to abolish or repeal.
[Often, one of the first acts of a dictator is to *abrogate* the powers of the press.]

appurtenance
ə purt´ nəns

n. An item of equipment; an accessory.
[The *appurtenances* that go with the apartment include an air conditioner and a washer/dryer combination.]

bivouac
bi´ və wak

n. A temporary camp or shelter.
[While following the Appalacian Trail, we looked for a sheltered, well-drained spot to set up our *bivouac*.]
bivouac *v.* To stay in cuch a camp.
[On June 30, Ewell's troops *bivouacked* near a road north of Gettysburg.]

cetacean
si tā´ shən

n. A member of the order of marine mammals that includes whales, dolphins, and porpoises.
[The blue whale is the largest of the cetaceans.]
cetacean or **cetaceous** *adj.*

decry
di krī´

v. To criticize strongly; to denounce.
[Many citizens of the world still *decry* the failure of stronger nations to intervene in the genocidal civil war that, in the 1990s, raged in Rwanda, Africa.]

desuetude
de´ swi tood

n. A state of disuse.
[The old factory building was rescued from *desuetude* by the city's conversion of it to attractive, affordable housing units.]

leviathan
li vī´ ə thən

n. Anything that is of enormous size.
[The cruise ship was a *leviatha*n with luxury accommodations for over two thousand passengers.]

mawkish
mô´ kish

adj. **1.** Excessively sentimental.
[Because today's greeting card verses are so *mawkish*, I often select a humorous one instead.]
2. Having an unpleasant, sickly sweet taste.
[The *mawkish* beverage tasted like coconut milk and overripe mango.]

misapprehend
mis a pri hen´ shən

v. To fail to understand correctly.
[So that no one *misapprehend*s the conditions of the agreement, let's put them in writing.]
misapprehension *n.*

parochial
pə rō′ kē əl

adj. **1.** Limited or narrow in scope or outlook.
[She is of the *parochial* view that what's good for her state is good for the whole country.]
2. Of or related to a church parish.
[You don't have to be a church member to teach at a *parochial* school.]

purvey
pər vā′

v. To be in the business of supplying goods, especially food or provisions, for use.
[The Loxley Company has *purveyed* bakery goods for five generations.]
purveyor   *n.*

recourse
rē′ kōrs

n. **1.** A turning to someone or something for aid.
[You have *recourse* to the courts if you cannot settle the dispute on your own.]
2. A source of help or support.
[Reading was his usual *recourse* during periods of insomnia.]

replete
ri plēt′

adj. Well supplied; full.
[His memoir is *replete* with amusing anecdotes.]

waive
wāv

v. To give up as a right; to forgo.
[The town *waived* a portion of property taxes for senior citizens.]
waiver   *n.*

8A Understanding Meanings

Read the sentences in each group below. If a sentence correctly uses the word in boldface, write C on the line of the corresponding number below the group. If a sentence is incorrect, rewrite it so that the vocabulary word in boldface is used correctly.

■   1. To be **replete** is to be abundantly filled.
2. A **cetacean** is a written summons to appear before a court.
3. An **aborigine** is a member of the original population of a place.
4. An **appurtenance** is a false appearance intended to deceive.
5. A **mawkish** taste is one that is sickeningly sweet.

1. _____

2. _____

3. _____

4. _____

5. _____

■ 6. **Recourse** is that which is turned to for help or support.
  7. To **bivouac** is to camp out.
  8. To **purvey** something is to criticize or condemn it.
  9. To **decry** is to speak in a loud, authoritative voice.
10. **Misapprehension** is a state of anxiety.

6. _____

7. _____

8. _____

9. _____

10. _____

■ 11. A **leviathan** is an amusing situation.
12. To **abrogate** a treaty is to ratify it.
13. **Parochial** authority is that which is exercised by a church parish.
14. **Desuetude** is a suspension of activity.
15. A **waiver** is a person who appears indecisive.

11. _____

12. _____

13. _____

14. _____

15. _____

8B Using Words

If the word (or a form of the word) in boldface fits in a sentence in the group below it, write the word in the blank space. If the word does not fit, leave the space empty.

1. **leviathan**
  (a) This transport plane, which can carry the bulk of our supplies in one trip, is the _____ of our fleet.
  (b) I hooked a good-sized _____ but it got away before I could land it.
  (c) The blue whale has been aptly named the _____ of the deep.

2. **purvey**
  (a) Carmen offered to _____ her car to me for five hundred dollars.
  (b) We _____ meats and meat products to most of the restaurants in the area.
  (c) Stall holders _____ hot pretzels with mustard to busy pedestrians.

3. **bivouac**
   (a) The hikers can _____ no more than fifteen miles a day.
   (b) We plan to _____ for the night in the pasture by Twelve-Tree Farm.
   (c) Scouts spotted smoke rising from the campfires of the enemy _____ .

4. **cetacean**
   (a) The killer whale is a predatory _____ that lives on fish and sea mammals.
   (b) _____ communication is highly evolved among dolphins.
   (c) The _____ is one of the largest members of the marine mammals.

5. **abrogate**
   (a) You cannot _____ this agreement without the consent of the cosigners.
   (b) I know that you are making that noise just to _____ me.
   (c) When I became a parent, I decided to _____ television completely.

6. **recourse**
   (a) You do have legal _____ ; you can appeal your case.
   (b) As the flood waters rose, we had _____ to a large rubber dinghy from the attic.
   (c) Can you _____ the route you took to get to the ballpark?

7. **misapprehend**
   (a) The police expect to _____ the suspects very soon.
   (b) How could you _____ a straightforward statement like "Just do it"?
   (c) We may _____ each other unless each of us listens carefully.

8. **mawkish**
   (a) The _____ display of first editions attracted serious book collectors to the exhibit.
   (b) I was offered a _____ brew made from cassava root sweetened with honey.
   (c) Unable to think of a reply, I maintained a somewhat _____ silence.

8C Synonyms, Antonyms, Analogies

Each group of four words below contains two words that are either synonyms or antonyms. Circle these two words; then circle the S if they are synonyms, the A if they are antonyms.

1. LEVIATHAN   CONFUSED
   ABORIGINAL   NATIVE   S   A

2. MAWKISH   OPEN-MINDED
   COVERT   PAROCHIAL   S   A

3. RECOURSE   WAIVER
   USEFULNESS   DESUETUDE   S   A

4. APPURTENANCE   BIVOUAC
   IMPLEMENT   OUTCOME   S   A

5. CLAIM   PURVEY
   WAIVE   DIGEST   S   A

Complete the analogies by selecting the pair of words whose relationship most resembles the relationship of the pair in capital letters. Circle the letter in front of the pair you choose.

6. SENTIMENTAL : MAWKISH ::
   (a) plain : variegated   (c) invigorating : stultifying
   (b) beneficent : insidious   (d) old-fashioned : antediluvian

7. BIVOUAC : TENT ::
   (a) wage : vendetta   (c) read : dissertation
   (b) swim : pool   (d) conduct : orchestra

8. LEVIATHAN : SIZE ::
   (a) iconoclast : awe   (c) valedictory : farewell
   (b) savant : knowledge   (d) fealty : loyalty

9. DOLPHIN : CETACEAN ::
   (a) turtle : aquatic   (c) monkey : primate
   (b) buffalo : bovine   (d) horse : equestrian

10. AMBIGUITY : MISAPPREHENSION ::
    (a) misbehavior : aberration   (c) tool : reparation
    (b) insult : animosity   (d) largesse : remuneration

8D Images of Words

Circle the letter of each sentence that suggests the numbered boldface vocabulary word. In each group, you may circle more than one letter or none at all

1. aborigine

(a) The first inhabitants of Australia arrived there from Asia 20,000 years ago.

(b) The Aserkoffs's ancestors came to America from Russia in 1902.

(c) In 1862, the source of the River Nile was traced to Lake Victoria in east central Africa.

2. decry

(a) Some fans maintain that the introduction of the aluminum bat has ruined baseball.

(b) From my window I could hear the raucous sound of gulls at the fish pier.

(c) "How can you discard items that could be donated to shelters for the homeless?"

3. replete

(a) Chaucer's *Canterbury Tales* is a wonderful collection of stories portraying fourteenth-century English society.

(b) We searched without success for the missing piece to the jigsaw puzzle.

(c) Before the National Marine Fisheries Service placed it on the endangered species list in 1995, coho salmon were abundant in the waters of the Pacific Northwest.

4. misapprehension

(a) He thought she said "End it," when what she actually said was "Mend it."

(b) This blue line on the map is a river, not a road.

(c) Elise was sure that there would be no final exam, but she was wrong.

5. abrogate

(a) The new tax regulations take effect on January 1.

(b) Ms. Alverez, chairwoman of the fund-raising campaign, insists that its success is due to the unflagging work of the volunteers.

(c) Since I took her to the vet, Mittens refuses to have anything to do with me.

6. cetacean

(a) Porpoises are blunt snouted.

(b) As you drive the route along the Everglades, you may see an alligator.

(c) My aquarium is contains intriguing, brightly colored tropical fish.

7. parochial

(a) My older step-brother has no interest in traveling—not abroad, not even to other parts of this country.

(b) What I like best about the school is the diversity among its students.

(c) There is no disputing the fact that the square root of 9 is 3.

8. waive

(a) The French cheered when they saw the tricolor fluttering from the mast.

(b) Students who live in this state do not have to pay the university's registration fee.

(c) Be sure to know what rights you are guaranteed by the Constitution so that you never unintentionally relinquish any of them.

9. desuetude

(a) A sedentary lifestyle can result in loss of bone density as one gets older.

(b) The art of letter writing, alas, has gone the way of the quill pen.

(c) Tourists can visit the ghost town of Jerome, Arizona, formerly a bustling mining town.

10. appurtenance

(a) What appeared to be a sea monster was actually a floating log.

(b) After Zoe unpacked her sketch pad, pencils, erasers, and easel, onlookers watched her capture the glee of the children splashing in the fountain.

(c) Cato's talk was full of archaic phrases like "prithee" and "gadzooks."

8E Narrative

Read the narrative below; then complete the exercise that follows it.

SAVE THE WHALES OR THE WHALERS?

Until European explorers first made contact with them in the early 1800s, the Inuit people were under the **misapprehension** that they were the only people in the world. Such a **parochial** view was understandable since they lived on the remote coast of northwest Greenland, eight hundred miles from the North Pole and five hundred miles from the nearest settlement to the south.

Life is not easy in a place as far north as Qaanaaq, an Inuit settlement close to the site of the first European contact. The sun disappears entirely during the long polar night from November to February, and temperatures drop to far below zero. Yet, the Inuit have survived for a thousand years in this inhospitable climate, ever since their ancestors, having crossed the Bering Strait into North America, spread eastward and reached Greenland about A.D. 1000.

They have been able to do so because the waters off Qaanaaq are **replete** with fish, thanks to warm ocean currents from the south, which are rich in nutrients. The fish attract a variety of sea mammals, chiefly seals and a species of small whales known as narwhals. For centuries, these creatures have provided the Inuit with food, clothing, oil, tools, shelter, and weapons. The skills of the hunters have allowed the Inuit to survive, with each generation passing the skills on to the next. Today, about five hundred Inuit live at Qaanaaq. Unlike other Eskimo groups in Siberia, Alaska, northern Canada, and the west coast of Greenland, whose survival skills have fallen into **desuetude** due to prolonged contact with European culture, the Inuit have preserved much of their way of life.

February marks the start of two months of twilight and the beginning of the hunting season. As soon as the weather permits, families leave Qaanaaq, traveling by dogsled to **bivouac** along the edge of the firm ice, where they hunt for seals, walruses, polar bears, and whales. During the hunting season, the Inuit kill up to two hundred narwhals, weighing as much as three thousand pounds apiece. They preserve the meat by packing it in ice. The skin, which contains vitamin C, an important benefit in a land where few plants grow, they eat raw or boiled.

Of course, Qaanaaq has not escaped outside influences. It has changed greatly in recent years and now has a post office, a school, a clinic, a food store, and even a **purveyor** of hotdogs at the Polar Grill. Its inhabitants no longer live in igloos but in houses with indoor plumbing, running hot water, oil-generated electricity, and other **appurtenances** of modern living. To the inhabitants who can find employment in other ways, killing whales from sea-going kayaks by harpoon, even when supplemented by high-powered rifles, has become unnecessary to their existence.

This view is echoed in the larger modern world. Many people today **decry** the killing of whales under any circumstances, but this was not always the case. Throughout much of the nineteenth century and well into the twentieth, commercial whalers hunted most species to the point of extinction in their quest for whale oil, which was used for lighting lamps. With the development of electricity, however, **cetacean** oil was no longer necessary. As time passed and their numbers decreased, these ocean **leviathans** began to have an almost mystical hold on the human imagination.

By mid century, whale conservationists, opposed to the indiscriminate slaughter of these intelligent marine mammals, had **recourse** to the International Whaling Commission (IWC). This is a voluntary organization of twenty-four whaling nations, formed in 1945 to set limits on the numbers of whales taken each year. When these quotas proved unrealistic and the depletion of stocks continued, activists, using the slogan "save the whale," persuaded the IWC to ban all whaling in 1986. An exception was made for "**aboriginal** subsistence whaling," a **waiver** that allowed the Inuit and a few other isolated groups to continue their hunting practices.

Since then, pro-whaling groups in countries that once prospered from whaling, notably Norway and Japan, have sought to have the ban **abrogated**. Members of these groups argue that the number of whales worldwide has grown to the point that these mammals are no longer endangered. They dismiss as **mawkish** nonsense the view that there is something special about whales that makes it immoral to kill them. To bolster their case, they point out that the Inuit use rifles to finish off the harpooned whales, which is hardly a traditional method. They charge that they also sell some of the meat, suggesting that this makes them commercial whalers. Using the same arguments, supporters of the ban would like to make it total, extending it to include the Inuit. The people of Qaanaaq, finding themselves caught in the middle, must sometimes wish they could turn back the clock to a time when they were all alone in the world.

Answer each of the following questions in a sentence. Whenever a vocabulary word does not appear in the question, try to use one (or a form of one) in your answer. In a few cases, both question and answer may contain vocabulary words.

1. Why are **cetaceans** an important part of Inuit life?

   _____

2. What **appurtenances** do the Inuit use when they hunt whales today that they did not use historically?

   _____

3. What criticism is made of those who oppose all whale hunting?

   _____

4. Why did the International Whaling Commission permit the Inuit to continue catching whales in spite of the ban of 1986?

   _____

5. How were the Inuit able to survive so far north for such a long time?

   _____

6. What are some areas of Inuit life that have not fallen into **desuetude?**

   _____

7. What issue is the International Whaling Commission facing with respect to its 1986 ban?

   _____

8. Do you think the Inuit should continue to receive a **waiver** from the ban on whaling? Explain your answer.

   _____

9. Why is it impossible for the Inuit to take a **parochial** view of the world today?

_____

10. What **recourse** do you think the Inuit have if they are banned from whaling by the IWC?

_____

WORDLY WISE

The Book of Psalms in the Old Testament makes reference to a huge sea monster that symbolizes evil: "Thou didst crush the heads of Leviathan." The word **leviathan** was popularized by the seventeenth-century philosopher Thomas Hobbes, in a work that took *Leviathan* as its title and described a vast state with total control over its hapless citizens. The word *leviathan* came to mean anything of great size, such as a whale or a great ship. The word also serves as a useful metaphor to describe that which terrifies by its great size and power, such as the Nazi party of Germany between 1933 and 1945.

Hidden Message

Write out, in the spaces provided to the right of each sentence, the words from lessons 5 through 8 that are missing in each of the sentences below. Be sure that the words you choose fit the meaning of each sentence and have the same number of letters as there are spaces. The number following each sentence gives the word list from which the missing word must be taken. If the exercise is done properly, the shaded boxes will spell out the answer to this question: "Why is experience such a hard teacher?"

1. A Native American is a(n) _____ . (8)

2. Nothing seems to rouse her from her _____ . (6)

3. It was a(n) _____ error to ignore the warning. (5)

4. Failing to appear will _____ his claim to damages. (7)

5. I did not _____ any of my rights in the matter. (8)

6. I _____ any attempt to label me a fraud. (8)

7. It's useless to _____ since we know all the facts. (5)

8. The Model T Ford was the _____ to the Model A. (6)

9. We will _____ this amount in the final total. (7)

10. The judge's _____ guarantees them a fair trial. (5)

11. The sun was formed from a(n) _____ mass of gases. (7)

12. Aids became _____ in East Africa in the 1990's. (6)

13. The _____ between Jews and Arabs persists. (7)

14. The dolphin is a(n) _____ , as is the whale. (8)

15. We easily saw through such an obvious _____ . (5)

16. A(n) _____ mare will produce many foals. (6)
17. The _____ plot to kill the king was foiled. (7)
18. It's time to get rid of this _____ system. (5)

19. This lever is designed to _____ the switch. (6)

20. His _____ took many forms but went unpunished. (5)
21. They ended their _____ with a handshake. (5)
22. Her _____ comments hurt my feelings. (7)

23. His _____ love poems were embarrassing to read. (8)
24. The _____ flower beds make an attractive display. (7)

25. These boring lectures _____ the mind. (5)
26. The machines left in _____ began to rust. (8)
27. The _____ consisted of twenty tents. (8)

28. Listening to his _____ voice depresses us. (6)
29. He has a(n) _____ interest in the firms' merger. (5)

30. This new vessel is the _____ of cruise ships. (8)
31. Rejection of moral values leads to _____ . (7)
32. H.R. & Co. _____ beef and beef products only. (8)

33. The guests, _____ after the meal, stayed late. (8)
34. He offered a(n) _____ of songs, skits, and jokes. (7)
35. His _____ toward foreigners upset his friends. (7)
36. We listened to them _____ as we tried to sleep. (5)
37. What _____ do I have if I change my mind. (8)
38. I.Q. tests measure a person's _____ abilities. (6)

39. The cows will not drink _____ water. (6)

40. Both parties must _____ the agreement. (7)

41. _____ is an important quality to look for in a friend. (5)

42. Basketball players may take Michael Jordan as their _____ . (7)

43. Many Russians _____ the evil deeds of Josef Stalin. (5)

44. A priest must _____ the devil and all his works. (7)

45. I felt like a(n) _____ when the members ignored me. (6)

46. The drug's hold on him was _____ , but finally total. (6)

Lesson 9

Word List

Study the definitions of the words below; then do the exercises for the lesson.

apposite
a´ pə zət

adj. Highly relevant; apt.
[The Chrysler Building in Manhattan is an *apposite* example of the skyscraper, an architectural wonder dating from the 1920s.]

calumny
ka´ ləm ne

n. A false accusation meant to hurt someone's reputation; slander.
[In those days, anyone commiting *calumny* was likely to be challenged to a duel by the injured party.]
calumnious *adj.*

domain
dō mān´

n. 1. An area or territory over which control is exercised.
[The *domain* of the Mongol conqueror Genghis Khan extended over much of Asia during the thirteenth-century.]
2. A field of activity, knowledge, or concern.
[In the *domain* of the arts, the Maya civilization (c. 600–c.1500) of Central America was extraordinarily advanced.]

dorsal
dôr´ səl

adj. Of, on, or near the back.
[The *dorsal* shell of a turtle is called the carapace.]

enervate
e´ nər vāt

v. To lessen the vigor or strength of; to enfeeble.
[Sitting too long in the hot whirlpool at her health club *enervated* my cousin.]

epicure
e´ pi kyoor

n. One with discriminating taste, especially but not exclusively relating to food and drink.
[*Epicures* gathered at Le Crillon in Paris to name the chef of the year.]

exculpate
ek´ skəl pāt

v. To clear from alleged guilt or fault.
[Through her diligence and knowledge of the law, the young attorney *exculpated* the defendant.]
exculpatory *adj.*

heterogeneous
he tə rə jē´ nē əs

adj. Differing in kind or parts; varied.
[The college students in this older neighborhood help make the community more *heterogeneous*.]

infinitesimal
in fi nə te´ sə məl

adj. Extremely small in size or quantity.
[Quarks are *infinitesimal* subatomic particles that make up protons and neutrons.]

lateral
la´ tə rəl

adj. Of, at, from, or towards the side.
[The tree assumed a more upright form once some of the *lateral* branches were removed.]

primeval
prī mē´ vəl

adj. Of or relating to the earliest ages; primitive.
[The dinosaur whose bones we uncovered may have died in a *primeval* swamp a hundred million years ago.]

84

quintessence kwin te´ səns	*n.* The best or most typical example. [Ballet dancer Vaslov Nijinsky (1890–1950) was said to be the *quintessence* of grace and beauty.] **quintessential** *adj.*
serrated sə rāt´ əd	*adj.* Having a saw-toothed or notched edge. [The linden tree has *serrated* leaves.]
veritable ver´ ə tə bəl	*adj.* Being, in fact, the thing named or described; literally so. Often used to emphasize the aptness of a metaphor. [The sound system failed, making the concert a *veritable* disaster.]
viviparous vī vi´ pə rəs	*adj.* Producing living young instead of eggs, in the manner of most mammals and some reptiles and fishes. [The duck-billed platypus of Australia and Tasmania is not *viviparous* even though it is a mammal.]

9A Understanding Meanings

Read the sentences in each group below. If a sentence correctly uses the word in boldface, write C on the line of the corresponding number below the group. If a sentence is incorrect, rewrite it so that the vocabulary word in boldface is used correctly.

■ 1. To **exculpate** someone is to find that person guilty.
  2. The **dorsal** area is the region along the back.
  3. A **serrated** edge is one that is saw-toothed.
  4. A **lateral** move is one made unexpectedly.
  5. An **apposite** title is one that fits.

  1. _____
  2. _____
  3. _____
  4. _____
  5. _____

■ 6. A **primeval** forest is one that existed in ancient times.
  7. A **heterogeneous** group is one whose members are all the same.
  8. **Calumny** is money paid in compensation for an injury.
  9. A **veritable** fortune is one that is truly a fortune.
  10. To **enervate** someone is to invigorate that person.

6. _____

7. _____

8. _____

9. _____

10. _____

■ 11. A **viviparous** creature is one that eats its victims alive.
  12. An **epicure** is one who pretends to be able to heal the sick.
  13. The **quintessence** of civility is civility in its purest form.
  14. An **infinitesimal** amount is one that is extremely small.
  15. A **domain** is a particular field of activity.

11. _____

12. _____

13. _____

14. _____

15. _____

9B Using Words

If the word (or a form of the word) in boldface fits in a sentence in the group below it, write the word in the blank space. If the word does not fit, leave the space empty.

1. **exculpate**
   (a) The manufacturers of the roller coaster were _____ because the rider who was injured had taken a crazy chance by standing up on the ride.
   (b) Before painting the storefront, we will have to _____ several layers of old paint.
   (c) "Just look at the evidence: it is definitely _____ ."

2. **quintessential**
   (a) It is _____ that Lucia gets this message without delay.
   (b) Jackson Pollock is a _____ painter of twentieth-century abstract expressionism.
   (c) Byron, Keats, and Shelley, those _____ romantic figures, wrote immortal poetry.

3. **domain**
   (a) Boolean algebra is not my _____ , so I must defer to your opinion.
   (b) The Louisiana Purchase greatly extended the _____ of the United States.
   (c) A recluse, Emily Dickinson's _____ was the upstairs of her Amherst home.

4. **veritable**

   (a) A _____ mountain of trash had piled up during the refuse collectors' strike.

   (b) The doctor's unflagging dedication to fighting the Ebola virus in Zaire made her a _____ hero.

   (a) Edna St. Vincent Millay's poem "The Courage That My Mother Had" is a _____ tribute of a daughter to her mother.

5. **infinitesimal**

   (a) The universe stretches for an _____ distance in all directions.

   (b) A trillion is so _____ a number that we cannot imagine it.

   (c) A millionth of a gram is an _____ amount.

6. **apposite**

   (a) Unfortunately, the brothers found themselves on _____ sides of the conflict.

   (b) The example you give is not _____ to the situation and should be disregarded.

   (c) Artist Norman Rockwell's magazine covers are _____ of an America that he imagined.

7. **epicure**

   (a) Someone who eats only at fast-food restaurants cannot be called an _____ .

   (b) She is a literary _____ who delights in Isaac Bashevis Singer's Nobel prize-winning narratives of Polish-Jewish culture.

   (c) The true _____ is willing to pay a high price for these Provencal truffles.

8. **primeval**

   (a) Archaeopteryx was a _____ bird that lived two hundred millions years ago.

   (b) A _____ number such as 13 can be divided only by itself and one.

   (c) Life on earth began in the _____ seas of three billion years ago.

9C Synonyms, Antonyms, Analogies

Each group of four words below contains two words that are either synonyms or antonyms. Circle these two words; then circle the S if they are synonyms, the A if they are antonyms.

| 1. | EXCULPATE | ABJURE | | |
| | ENERVATE | ENLIVEN | S | A |

| 2. | VERITABLE | INFINITESIMAL | | |
| | TORPID | ENORMOUS | S | A |

3. DOMAIN   TERRITORY
    CALUMNY   GENEALOGY   S   A

4. SMOOTH   PRIMEVAL
    SERRATED   INCHOATE   S   A

5. EXCULPATORY   PRIMEVAL
    INCRIMINATING   CONTENTIOUS   S   A

Complete the analogies by selecting the pair of words whose relationship most resembles the relationship of the pair in capital letters. Circle the letter in front of the pair you choose.

6. CALUMNY : ENCOMIUM ::
    (a) desuetude : idleness   (c) protagonist : antagonist
    (b) chicanery : rectitude   (d) precursor : acolyte

7. DORSAL : LATERAL ::
    (a) front : rear   (c) right : left
    (b) inside : outside   (d) back : side

8. EPICURE : TASTE ::
    (a) athlete : sport   (c) Olympian : skill
    (b) dancer : grace   (d) dissembler : falsehood

9. APPOSITE : GERMANE ::
    (a) apparent : indubitable   (c) relevant : pertinent
    (b) quintessential : nonpareil   (d) mawkish : derisive

10. HETEROGENEOUS : VARIEGATED ::
    (a) intrinsic : inherent   (c) defoliate : exfoliate
    (b) intractable : uniform   (d) explicit : implicit

9D Images of Words

Circle the letter of each sentence that suggests the numbered boldface vocabulary word. In each group, you may circle more than one letter or none at all.

1. dorsal
(a) A small shed had been built onto the back of the house.
(b) You must turn to the back of the book to find the footnotes.
(c) The upper surface of the trout is speckled in contrast to its pale belly.

2. calumny

(a) The neighbor maintained, without a shred of supporting evidence, that the parents were neglecting their child.

(b) An earthquake followed by a fire was almost too much to be borne.

(c) He is a man of such integrity that I cannot believe what you have just said about him.

3. viviparous

(a) American dramatist Wendy Wasserstein has been writing successful plays for over twenty years.

(b) The children become quite lively once they are allowed outside to play.

(c) The elephant calf was upright and able to walk less than an hour after its birth.

4. lateral

(a) My appointment to the position of sales director was neither a promotion nor a demotion.

(b) The ball was thrown directly above the player's head.

(c) The ribs of vertebrates are attached to either side of the spine.

5. heterogeneous

(a) The United States is made up of people from all over the world.

(b) The camp attracted young people from a variety of neighborhoods.

(c) Hannah Arendt's report on the trial of Adolf Eichmann was brilliant and controversial.

6. enervate

(a) The din in the room made it impossible for me to think clearly.

(b) The fever left the patient barely able to sit up in bed.

(c) With little notice she courageously took on the part and played it with grate élan.

7. domain

(a) My brother can't enter my room without my permission.

(b) Growing up on the farm in Nebraska has given me cherished memories.

(c) In this pride of lions, one female is the leader.

8. quintessence

(a) Our five senses give us information about the external world.

(b) The Zen master's years of meditation made him a vision of calm.

(c) One part juice concentrate is diluted with four parts water.

9. serrated

(a) A series of V-shaped notches had been cut into the top of the fence.

(b) It is difficult to cut the meat with a knife with a smooth-edged blade.

(c) We were jolted up and down as we rode our bikes along the cobbled streets.

10. exculpate

(a) In *The Scarlet Letter*, Hester Prynne refused to identify her adulterous partner.

(b) Margot took whole passages from the book and passed them off as her work.

(c) There was no way for the animal to escape from the trap.

9E Narrative   *Read the narrative below; then complete the exercise that follows it.*

WHITE DEATH

The **enervating** heat of the South Australian summer sent hordes of people to the beach where they found relief by swimming in the Indian Ocean. Shirley Ann Durdin was one of them. She almost certainly had no presentiment of danger. All she probably felt was a violent shove before the water around her turned red and she was gone, the hapless victim of a great white shark.

Almost immediately, a **veritable** navy of shark hunters took to their boats, armed with guns, harpoons, nets, and poisoned bait in a futile attempt to track down the killer and avenge Durdin's death. Although the attack occurred in 1985, the description of how it happened is characteristic of many shark attacks.

For centuries, humans have viewed the great white shark as the **quintessence** of evil, a remorseless killer that goes after humans out of sheer malevolence. The sight of its **dorsal** fin slicing through the water sends shivers down the spine. In Australia, it is known as white death, a name that many believe is **apposite**. **Calumny** of the white shark has only increased in the last several years, especially in movies. Even though sharks appeared in the earth's **primeval** sea three hundred million years ago, we still know very little about these creatures.

The great white shark has unique qualities that allow it to surprise, dominate, and overcome its prey—usually large marine animals, fish, and sea turtles. From fifteen to twenty feet in length and weighing a ton and a half or more, its powerful jaws are large enough to swallow a sea lion or a human child in one gulp. Its **serrated** teeth, three inches long, are arranged in rows, and when it loses one another moves forward to replace it. Its brain receives information through an array of unusual sensory capabilities. A shark's olfactory sense is extremely acute. It can smell blood in concentrations as low as one part per ten million, allowing it to locate a site with blood from miles away. Through a row of **lateral** sensors on each side of its body, it is able to feel the irregular vibrations made by an injured fish or the arms and legs of a swimmer. It also possesses a sense that humans lack. Through receptors under its snout, it can detect the **infinitesimally** small electrical field, as low as one hundred-millionth of a volt, given off by all living creatures. This too allows it to locate prey in its watery **domain** from a significant distance.

Although the word *shark* evokes an image of the great white, that creature is just one of about 350 different species. They comprise an extremely **heterogeneous** group, from the six-inch dwarf shark to the fifty-foot, plankton-eating whale shark. Only about a dozen species have been known to attack humans, including the tiger shark, the bull shark, the hammerhead, the whitetip, the blue shark, as well as the most feared of them all, the great white shark.

If humans have reason to fear sharks, sharks have even more reason to fear humans. From seventy to one hundred shark attacks are reported worldwide each year, of which from five to fifteen are fatal; in contrast, millions of sharks are caught annually through the use of long-line fishing gear, intended for other fish. While rarely successful as a food for humans because of the high level of uric acid in their flesh, sharks in recent years have been killed for their fins, which are an essential ingredient in shark-fin soup. This is a popular dish in some Asian countries. In Hong Kong, **epicures** pay as much as fifty dollars for a bowl of this delicacy.

Unlike other fish, which lay thousands of eggs at a time, sharks are **viviparous** and bear from five to ten pups at a time with possibly two years between litters. Given this slow rate of reproduction, along with the increased attacks upon it, the shark population is declining. To do nothing to reverse this would be a tragedy, for sharks play an important part in maintaining a healthy balance in the oceans. In addition, researchers have learned that sharks do not seem to develop tumors. Speculating that sharkskin or its derivatives could play an important role in treating some cancers, scientists would like to have more opportunities to work with sharks.

Responding to concerns that the great white shark is disappearing, South Africa declared it an endangered species in 1991. Since then California, Australia, and Tasmania have joined them. At the April 2000 conference on endangered species, the United States asked that the great white shark be placed in the most protected category. While humans may not yet be ready to **exculpate** the shark, they seem to realize the species needs safeguarding.

Answer each of the following questions in a sentence. Whenever a vocabulary word does not appear in the question, try to use one (or a form of one) in your answer. In a few cases, both question and answer may contain vocabulary words.

1. Is it **apposite** to describe all sharks as dangerous to humans? Explain your answer.

_____

2. In its **domain,** why is the great white shark such a successful predator?

_____

3. How do you know that sharks have existed on earth longer than humans have?

_____

4. Why have **epicures** never been interested in shark meat?

_____

5. What details in the narrative illustrate the statement that sharks are a **heterogeneous** group?

_____

6. What do a saw and a great white shark's tooth have in common?

_____

7. Why might even a small cut on a swimmer attract a great white shark to that person?

_____

8. What warning might people have that a shark is in the water nearby?

_____

9. How do sharks differ from other fish in the way they reproduce?

_____

10. What are some of the causes of the **calumny** directed toward sharks?

_____

11. Why would it be accurate to say there has been a **veritable** decimation of sharks in the last few decades?

_____

WORDLY WISE

The Greek philosopher Epicurus (341–270 B.C.) taught that pleasure, which he defined as freedom from pain and anxiety, was the highest, indeed, the only good. He did not, however, advocate a life of unbridled pleasure with no restraints, but rather one that was lived in strict accordance with ascetic principles. In the centuries that followed, Epicurus's teachings were distorted, and an **epicure** came to mean one who indulged in pleasures of the senses. Still later, the word became refined until it acquired its present meaning, "one who shows refinement of taste, especially in matters of food and drink."

In ancient and medieval times, it was believed that all things were made from just four substances, called *essences* (from the Latin verb *esse*, "to be.") These four essences were earth, air, fire, and water. In addition, there was believed to be a fifth essence, called the **quintessence** (from the Latin *quintus*, "fifth") that permeated all of nature and the heavens. It was the purest and most concentrated essence. This seemingly far-fetched idea gave us the word *quintessential*.

Lesson 10

Word List

Study the definitions of the words below; then do the exercises for the lesson.

acumen
a´ kyə mən

n. Keenness of the mind; shrewdness.
[Kimba Wood's legal *acumen* led to her nomination for a position on the Supreme Court.]

apotheosis
ə pä thē ō´ səs

n. **1.** The elevation of a person or thing to divine status.
[Nero's vanity was so great that nothing less than his *apotheosis* by the Roman senate could satisfy it.]
2. The highest point or best example.
[Many people view Beethoven's music as the *apotheosis* of the Romantic movement.]

askew
ə skyōo´

adj. and *adv.* Turned or twisted to one side; out of line.
[The gate to the cow pasture had been knocked slightly *askew* and didn't close properly.]

chasten
chā´ sən

v. To correct or improve by disciplining; to cause to be more careful or restrained.
[The boy's parents *chastened* him for arriving home after his curfew.]
chastening *adj.* Having the effect of humbling or restraining.

demarcation
dē mär kā´ shən

n. **1.** The act or process of setting a boundary; the boundary itself.
[According to the 1953 armistice, the DMZ (Demilitarized Zone) is the *demarcation* between North Korea and South Korea]
2. Separation; distinction.
[In the summer haze, there was no clear line of *demarcation* between sea and sky.]

dictum
dik´ təm

n. A statement or pronouncement.
[The gym instructor's *dictum* was "No pain, no gain."]

erstwhile
ərst´ wīl

adj. Of an earlier time; former.
[My *erstwhile* companions have all gone their separate ways.]

forte
fôr´ tā

n. An activity at which a person excels.
[Tennessee Williams was a poet and short story writer, but his *forte* was playwriting.]

habitué
hə bi´ chə wa

n. A person who regularly goes to a particular place.
[Edward Hopper painted the *habitués* of all-night diners.]

nonplus
nän pləs´

v. To cause to be at a loss as to what to say or do.
[The guest's continuing reticence *nonplussed* the host of the TV talk show.]

peripatetic
per ə pə te´ tik

adj. Of or relating to going from place to place, especially on foot.
[These *peripatetic* discussions among the lawyers took place between their offices and the courthouse.]

prodigal
prä´ di gəl

n. One who spends lavishly or wastefully.
[During the Gilded Age of the second half of the nineteenth-century, millionaires in the United States were often referred to as *prodigals*.]
prodigal *adj.*

sycophant
si´ kə fənt

n. One who uses flattery to win favor or to ingratiate him- or herself.
[The Emperor's *sycophant*s would not dream of telling him the truth about his "new clothes."]
sycophantic *adj.*

vacuous
va´ kyə wəs

adj. Lacking intelligence or ideas; intellectual emptiness.
[I couldn't wait to leave the dinner because of the *vacuous* conversation at the table.]

wraith
rāth

n. A shadowy or ghostlike figure.
[In the film, a *wraith* appeared out of the mist, pointed an accusing finger, and then was gone.]
wraithlike *adj.*

10A Understanding Meanings

Read the sentences in each group below. If a sentence correctly uses the word in boldface, write C on the line of the corresponding number below the group. If a sentence is incorrect, rewrite it so that the vocabulary word in boldface is used correctly.

■ 1. A **dictum** is a formal statement of principle.
    2. A **wraith** is a great rage or fury.
    3. To **chasten** someone is to discipline that person.
    4. **Apotheosis** is the raising of a person to high status.
    5. An **erstwhile** decision is one that was made previously.

1. _____

2. _____

3. _____

4. _____

5. _____

■ 6. A **sycophant** is an awkward or clumsy person.
    7. A **habitué** is one who frequents a particular establishment.
    8. **Demarcation** is the process of setting limits.
    9. A **nonplussed** person is one who is uncommitted.
   10. To be **askew** is to be dazed or stunned.

6. _____

7. _____

8. _____

9. _____

10. _____

■ 11. A **forte** is an activity at which a person excels.
  12. A **prodigal** is a highly gifted child.
  13. **Acumen** is quickness in understanding and dealing with a situation.
  14. A **vacuous** suggestion is one that is devoid of good sense.
  15. A **peripatetic** beggar is one who occupies a favorite spot.

11. _____

12. _____

13. _____

14. _____

15. _____

10B Using Words

If the word (or a form of the word) in boldface fits in a sentence in the group below it, write the word in the blank space. If the word does not fit, leave the space empty.

1. **askew**
   (a) The edge of the beach umbrella hit my hat and knocked it _____ .
   (b) All of the objects in the painting were _____ , giving it an unsettling appearance.
   (c) The bolt had been put in _____ , stripping the thread.

2. **apotheosis**
   (a) Liza was encouraged to hear the nurse practitioner's _____ for her case.
   (b) The Greek sculptor Praxiteles portrayed Aphrodite as the _____ of female beauty.
   (c) The _____ of their emperor was taken for granted by the Japanese people.

3. **nonplus**
   (a) I was _____ to discover myself in the subway headed in the wrong direction.
   (b) Please don't _____ the candidate by asking him personal questions.
   (c) The singer was so _____ by the audience's enthusiasm that she sang another encore.

4. **acumen**
   (a) Because Bruce works out every day, his physical _____ is exceptional.
   (b) She has never lost an election, so we shouldn't underestimate her political _____ .
   (c) Amman's musical _____ has made him a popular performer.

5. **erstwhile**
   (a) The _____ shoe factory was now a bustling shopping mall.
   (b) I remember Providence from an _____ visit several years ago.
   (c) The _____ Latin teacher now runs a "Fortune 500" company.

6. **vacuous**
   (a) The _____ pursuits of the newest millionaires were the subject of a scathing article in this month's business journal.
   (b) She showed me his _____ purse when I asked how much money she had.
   (c) The child's _____ stare was a sign of her complete exhaustion.

7. **chasten**
   (a) The arbitrator will _____ the two sides until they reach agreement.
   (b) It may be necessary to _____ Malcolm if he continues to disregard his sister's feelings.
   (c) The principal was able to _____ students without humiliating them.

8. **prodigal**
   (a) When Blanca first gets her allowance, she is a _____ spender.
   (b) I had the most _____ piece of good luck the other day.
   (c) William is a tennis _____ .

10C Synonyms, Antonyms, Analogies

Each group of four words below contains two words that are either synonyms or antonyms. Circle these two words; then circle the S if they are synonyms, the A if they are antonyms.

1. ALERT   VACUOUS
   FECUND   PRODIGAL   S   A

2. PERIPATETIC   STATIONARY
   INCHOATE   ERSTWHILE   S   A

3. ASKEW   DOLOROUS
   FRUGAL   PRODIGAL   S   A

4. STRATAGEM   DICTUM
   ACUMEN   CLEVERNESS   S   A

5. ASKEW   WRAITHLIKE
    CROOKED   MAWKISH   S   A

Complete the analogies by selecting the pair of words whose relationship most resembles the relationship of the pair in capital letters. Circle the letter in front of the pair you choose.

6. SYCOPHANT : FLATTERY ::
    (a) interloper : suspicion   (c) dancer : music
    (b) charlatan : guile   (d) savant : knowledge

7. ERSTWHILE : PROSPECTIVE ::
    (a) present : absent   (c) former : latter
    (b) actual : putative   (d) past : future

8. APOTHEOSIS : QUINTESSENTIAL ::
    (a) catharsis : hypothetical   (c) poverty : frugal
    (b) bigot : intolerant   (d) praise : essential

9. FENCE : DEMARCATION ::
    (a) IQ : intelligence   (c) line : boundary
    (b) gravestone : grave   (d) enclosure : wall

10. HABITUÉ : DENIZEN ::
    (a) charlatan : tycoon   (c) cohort : confidante
    (b) mogul : magnate   (d) neophyte : convert

10D Images of Words

Circle the letter of each sentence that suggests the numbered boldface vocabulary word. In each group, you may circle more than one letter or none at all.

1. **apotheosis**
(a) In the twelfth century, Queen Eleanor's court at Poitiers thronged with musicians and poets.
(b) The Egyptian god-king Khufu built the Great Pyramid for his tomb.
(c) Roger Bannister ran the first four-minute mile in 1954.

2. **forte**
(a) Arthur Ashe's backhand was especially feared by his opponents.
(b) Ray was an excellent chef; his desserts were his specialty.
(c) Mrs. Worthington insists that her daughter excels in everything she tries.

3. wraith

(a) The child claimed to have no parents and was looking for a place to sleep.

(b) A dim, shadowy figure emerged from the darkness and came toward us.

(c) Anita dressed herself in an old sheet for the masquerade.

4. peripatetic

(a) The doctor was accompanied by students as she went from ward to ward lecturing loudly.

(b) Mr. Ginsberg sets off every morning at seven to walk briskly around the block.

(c) I thought Carmilla was going to faint when she heard that Jonas was alive.

5. demarcation

(a) The captain asked passengers to leave the ship no later than 2 P.M.

(b) During the game, the children used chalk on the sidewalk to show each group's territory.

(c) Workers installed a velvet rope in the aisle between the front and back of the orchestra.

6. sycophantic

(a) Ms. Bruni was the governor's constant companion, praising his every thought.

(b) Because she was new in school, Fiona tried hard to be friendly.

(c) Dr. Lopez assured Mr. Rowley that the antibiotic would treat his infected foot.

7. dictum

(a) Professors knew that the history department's motto was "Publish or perish."

(b) Emerson said, "A foolish consistency is the hobgoblin of little minds . . . . "

(c) The sign over the door said, "Reminder: The last bus leaves at 11 P.M."

8. habitué

(a) Francesca is trying to stop biting her nails.

(b) Jean-Paul Sartre stopped in at the Deux Magots almost every day.

(c) Even though his wife would like to move to the city, Sam still prefers rural life.

9. nonplus

(a) Seven and thirteen are twenty, not nineteen.

(b) There was stunned silence when the director told the cast she was leaving the show.

(c) Angelica announced that she completed the *Times* crossword puzzle in ten minutes.

10. acumen

(a) By combining our savings, the three of us had just enough money to buy the car.

(b) My grandmother made a lot of money in the stock market through constant analysis and assessment.

(c) After months of study, Harry made it to the national spelling bee finals.

10E Narrative

Read the narrative below; then complete the exercise that follows it.

THE TYCOON OF POP

When the Andy Warhol Museum opened in 1994 in Pittsburgh, Pennsylvania, it marked the **apotheosis** of one of America's best-known and most prolific artists. Two characteristics are essential for a museum devoted to a single artist to be successful; if the artist is relatively obscure, few people will visit the museum, and if his or her output is small, there will be insufficient works to fill the space. Warhol succeeded triumphantly in both respects—he was both well-known and prolific. Each year thousands of people visit the museum, which displays only a portion of Warhol's prodigious output—more than three thousand works of art.

Pittsburgh was an appropriate choice for the museum. Warhol, whose parents had immigrated to the United States from Transylvania, grew up in one of its suburbs. After attending that city's Carnegie Institute of Technology, he graduated in 1949, at the age of twenty-one, with a degree in pictorial design and moved to New York City. Within a decade of his arrival in New York, through a combination of business **acumen** and his skill as a commercial artist, he earned enough money to buy an elegant Manhattan townhouse.

Having established himself financially, Andy Warhol wanted to make himself known as an artist. He set about blurring the **demarcation** that separated commercial art from fine art. Through the use of silk screen and photography, which allowed the creation of multiple copies of a work, and through the choice of common and often commercial objects as subject matter, he created art that expressed the reality of everyday life. This was in direct contrast to the art of the time, known as abstract expressionism. The work of Warhol and others was called popular art, later shortened to pop art.

Then Andy Warhol went further. His **forte** was self-promotion, and despite his putative indifference to fame, he pursued it avidly. Soon after his arrival in New York, he had begun to dye his hair silver, which accentuated his already **wraithlike** appearance. By the sixties, as he began to bald, he started wearing a silver wig, which strongly resembled a mop. This was to become a trademark. He went out almost every evening—to gallery openings, parties, restaurants, and clubs. He made a point of meeting celebrities and began associating with the elite of New York society, most of whom were flattered to be seen in his company. His seemingly **vacuous** gaze took in everything; his slight build belied his influence in the art world. Warhol's life and art became one: he himself became one of his greatest creations.

Warhol produced his art in a studio he called "the Factory." The name was apposite because of the techniques of mass production that he employed. The Factory changed its location a few times over the years but always attracted a small band of **sycophants** from the fringes of the art world and the drug culture, who were drawn there by Warhol's celebrity. The more outrageous their behavior, the more likely they were to gain admittance to his presence. In 1968, this led to tragedy when one of the Factory's former **habitués**, in a deranged state, shot and nearly killed Warhol. His celebrated **dictum** that in the future everyone will be world famous for fifteen minutes became true for him in a way he had not predicted.

Chastened by this experience, Warhol adopted a more cautious way of living, installing security cameras in the Factory for the first time. He dropped many of his **erstwhile** acquaintances. His prodigious output continued unabated. Paintings of soup cans, sculptures of soap-pad containers, multiple images of such celebrities as Marilyn Monroe, Jacqueline Kennedy, Elvis Presley, and, of course, portraits of himself with his silver wig **askew** became icons of pop art; all commanded high prices.

With his vast wealth, Warhol indulged himself by shopping on a **prodigal** scale for everything from old masters to cookie jars. His **peripatetic** expeditions took him to Manhattan art galleries, auction houses, jewelry stores, and flea markets, with a limousine following behind to transport the purchases to his twenty-room mansion.

Warhol died unexpectedly in 1987, following gallbladder surgery. His estate was valued at over a half-billion dollars, most of which he left to establish a foundation to promote the visual arts. The contents of his townhouse realized twenty-five million dollars at auction. His collection of 175 cookie jars sold for an average of fifteen hundred dollars each, a bargain to the proud owners, who could point thereafter to their genuine Warhol cookie jars.

During his lifetime, art critics disagreed on whether Warhol was a great artist or merely a self-promoter in a class by himself. Many refused to take his work seriously, and they were **nonplussed** when he agreed with them. When told that critics accused him of producing meaningless art, Andy Warhol's disarming response was, "They're right." Nevertheless, today, his influence is still present.

Answer each of the following questions in a sentence. Whenever a vocabulary word does not appear in the question, try to use one (or a form of one) in your answer. In a few cases, both question and answer may contain vocabulary words.

1. What talents did Warhol possess that helped him achieve success?

   _____

2. How did Warhol's physical appearance belie his importance in the art world?

   _____

3. What details suggest that Warhol was not concerned with a neat appearance?

_____

4. Why did Warhol become a **habitué** of the gatherings of celebrities and of New York society?

_____

5. What effect did the attempted assassination have on Warhol?

_____

6. Why do you think people were **sycophantic** toward Warhol?

_____

7. Why did Warhol's death leave many people **nonplussed**?

_____

8. What posthumous event extended Warhol's fame?

_____

9. In what way did Warhol's **prodigal** shopping trips actually increase his wealth?

_____

10. How did Warhol contradict his famous **dictum**?

_____

11. How was Warhol's art different from the art produced in the mid-twentieth century?

_____

WORDLY WISE

A person who possesses **acumen** could be said to have a sharp mind, and the etymology of the term suggests this. It comes from the Latin *acuere*, "to sharpen." Several other words share this root. An acute pain is one that is sharp, as is an acute angle. An acrid smell is one that feels sharp to the nose. Acids, too, have a sharp taste or smell. Acupuncture is an ancient Chinese medical treatment in which thin, sharp needles puncture the skin at carefully selected locations.

The Greek philosopher Artistotle gave instruction to his pupils as he walked about his school outside Athens. The Greek word **Peripatetic**, from *peri-*, "around," and *patein*, "to walk," became applied to his philosophy. The word has been retained, but without the capital *p* its meaning has become "traveling from place to place on foot."

Lesson 11

Word List

Study the definitions of the words below; then do the exercises for the lesson.

cacophony
ka kä´ fə nē

n. Harsh or jarring sound.
[A *cacophony* of sirens heralded the approach of the fire engines.]
cacophonous *adj.*

confrere
kän´ frer

n. Comrade; colleague.
[After her class in computer graphics, Tara gathered with her *confreres* to refine their plans for the required group project.]

convoke
kən vōk´

v. To summon or call together for a meeting.
[On December 10, 1948, the member states of the United Nations, who had been *convoked* to consider the Universal Declaration of Human Rights, voted overwhelmingly to adopt this document.]
convocation *n.*

filial
fi´ lē əl

adj. Of, relating to, or befitting a son or daughter.
[The ancient Chinese philosopher Confucius taught the importance of cultivating virtues such as righteousness, integrity, and *filial* piety.]

fractious
frak´ shəs

adj. Tending to be troublesome; irritable.
[What may appear to be simply *fractious* behavior in a child may actually be a symptom of parental neglect.]

fulminate
fool´ mə nāt

v. To express with denunciation, often in an explosive way.
["This is not fair to my workers!" the angry foreman *fulminated*.]
fulmination *n.*

jocular
jä´ kyə lər

adj. Given to or characterized by joking; playful; jolly.
[The children laughed with delight at the appearance of Santa Claus, with his *jocular* "Ho, Ho, Ho!"]
jocularity *n.*

nugatory
noo´ gə tōr ē

adj. Having no force or effect.
[Gyro's cynicism was made *nugatory* by Alexandra's irrepressible spirit.]

obloquy
ä´ blə kwē

n. 1. An utterance of denunciation.
[In 1961 the building of the Berlin Wall, which partitioned the city and imprisoned West German citizens within its boundaries, provoked public *obloquy*.]
2. The condition of one who is held in contempt for a shameful action.
[Having been seduced by false values, the antihero of the play becomes the victim of his own *obloquy*.]

palpable
pal´ pə bəl

adj. 1. Easy to touch or feel.
[The small but *palpable* lump on her arm was diagnosed as a cyst.]
2. Easy to see, hear, or recognize; obvious.
[There was a *palpable* tension in the room as the parents waited for the outcome of the operation on their child.]

parity
par´ ə tē

n. Equality of rank or value.
[The strengthening United States dollar eventually reached *parity* with the British pound.]

peruse
pə rōōz´

v. To read through something, either casually or closely.
[The amazing fact is that most Hollywood studios *perused* and rejected the filmstrip for *Star Wars*, the science-fiction film that, as it turned out, mesmerized audiences everywhere.]

polemic
pə le´ mik

n. **1.** An argument to refute a position or opinion.
[The protestor delivered a fiery *polemic* against the company's hiring practices, which she viewed as sexist.]
2. One who aggressively advocates a position.
[Anyone debating such an accomplished *polemic* would need keen rhetorical skills.]
polemical *adj.*
polemicist *n.*

supplicate
sə´ plə kāt

v. To ask for humbly; to plead or beg.
[The defendant *supplicated* the jury for compassion.]
supplicant *n.* One who pleads.
supplication *n.* A plea.

temporize
tem´ pə rīz

v. To act evasively in order to achieve a compromise or to gain time.
[Unwilling to vote the measure up or down, Congress *temporized*.]

11A Understanding Meanings

Read the sentences in each group below. If a sentence correctly uses the word in boldface, write C on the line of the corresponding number below the group. If a sentence is incorrect, rewrite it so that the vocabulary word in boldface is used correctly.

1. A **fractious** animal is one that is not easily controlled.
2. A **palpable** error is one that is impossible to cover up.
3. A **supplicant** is one who moves with ease and grace.
4. A **convocation** is an assembly of people called together.
5. A **polemicist** is one skilled in arguing a position.

1. _____

2. _____

3. _____

4. _____

5. _____

■ 6. **Obloquy** is the expression of grief for one who has died.
7. A **cacophonous** rendition is one that is unpleasantly loud and discordant.
8. To **temporize** is to act swiftly.
9. **Parity** is the state of being equal in value or importance.
10. A **filial** relationship is one between close friends.

6. _____

7. _____

8. _____

9. _____

10. _____

■ 11. To **fulminate** is to suffer in silence.
12. A **nugatory** matter is one to which attention must be paid.
13. To **peruse** a column is to read it thoroughly.
14. A **confrere** is a colleague.
15. **Jocularity** is lighthearted jesting.

11. _____

12. _____

13. _____

14. _____

15. _____

11B Using Words

If the word (or a form of the word) in boldface fits in a sentence in the group below it, write the word in the blank space. If the word does not fit, leave the space empty.

1. **polemic**
    (a) Colonist Thomas Paine's article was a _____ against English rule.
    (b) The child had a fit of _____ when told it was time to leave.
    (c) The debate consisted of stale _____ that changed the views of neither side.

2. **nugatory**
    (a) The agreement is _____ unless both parties signed it of their own accord.
    (b) The article is so one-sided that its value is _____ .
    (c) I pleaded with the manager to reconsider, but her response was _____ .

3. **confrere**

   (a) The chairwoman is meeting with her _____ to choose a successor.

   (b) The lawyer held a brief _____ with his client before addressing the judge.

   (c) The _____ at the National Assembly were all well known to each other.

4. **palpable**

   (a) To accuse such an upstanding citizen of dishonesty is a _____ absurdity.

   (b) The planes overhead set off a _____ vibration in the air.

   (c) The wraith seemed so _____ , yet it passed through a solid wall.

5. **supplicate**

   (a) Please _____ this assignment and give a copy to each student.

   (b) Street beggars _____ passing tourists to give them money.

   (c) We did our best to _____ the woman who was grieving the loss of her dog.

6. **obloquy**

   (a) Jeanne d'Arc did not deserve the _____ heaped upon her at the trial.

   (b) The senator delivered an hour-long _____ in support of the measure.

   (c) The _____ for our friend who died unexpectedly will be held on Saturday.

7. **convoke**

   (a) The king plans to _____ a meeting of the barons to settle their differences.

   (b) You cannot make a solemn promise and then _____ it for no good reason.

   (c) The goddess Demeter _____ Hades, King of the Underworld, to return her kidnapped daughter.

8. **peruse**

   (a) We drove so fast that I had no time to _____ the street signs.

   (b) The lookout was unable to _____ the approaching ship because of the fog.

   (c) The prenuptial agreement is a complicated one, and I will need time to _____ it.

11C Synonyms, Antonyms, Analogies

1. VERITABLE   MELODIOUS
   PALPABLE   CACOPHONOUS   S   A

2. DEMAND   SUPPLICATE
   DELAY   TEMPORIZE   S   A

3. DISMISS   CONVOKE
   OBVIATE   PERUSE   S   A

4. JOCULAR   COGNITIVE
   FILIAL   SOLEMN   S   A

5. SUPPLICATE   PLEAD
   CONVOKE   DECRY   S   A

Complete the analogies by selecting the pair of words whose relationship most resembles the relationship of the pair in capital letters. Circle the letter in front of the pair you choose.

6. CHIDE : FULMINATE ::
   (a) sell : purvey   (c) accept : eschew
   (b) explain : expatiate   (d) reward : punish

7. PALPABLE : TOUCH ::
   (a) amorphous : shape   (c) visual : sight
   (b) cacophonous : sound   (d) cognitive : understanding

8. READ : PERUSE ::
   (a) say : declaim   (c) actuate : terminate
   (b) eschew : embrace   (d) implicate : exculpate

9. PARITY : INEQUALITY ::
   (a) avocation : vocation   (c) disparity : similarity
   (b) integrity : probity   (d) alacrity : velocity

10. FRACTIOUS : RECALCITRANT ::
    (a) feckless : nugatory   (c) mawkish : articulate
    (b) heroic : brave   (d) criminal : illicit

11D Images of Words

Circle the letter of each sentence that suggests the numbered boldface vocabulary word. In each group, you may circle more than one letter or none at all.

1. jocularity
(a) The audience laughed when the speaker mispronounced the host's name.
(b) "I'll be with you forthwith unless I'm late; then I'll be with you fifthwith."
(c) "Did you enjoy your trip?" he said as I stumbled over a loose board.

2. cacophony
(a) The people in the cars screamed as the roller coaster plunged down the track.
(b) The ball of yarn was so tangled that we could not unravel it.
(c) Drivers leaned on their horns as the traffic grew worse by the minute.

3. supplicate
(a) "Please don't ignore our plight."
(b) "You'll be so glad you did this!"
(c) "We took so long to make up our minds that now it's too late."

4. parity
(a) Each side in the contest had the skill to defeat the other.
(b) In a utopia, each person would have the same rights as everyone else.
(c) All three clocks struck the hour at precisely the same moment.

5. temporize
(a) The company is no longer hiring full-time help.
(b) His motto was "Never do today what you can put off until tomorrow."
(c) Her reasonable words had the desired effect of calming the agitated group.

6. nugatory
(a) Every member is required to attend the meeting.
(b) The deep snow made the mountain trails impassable.
(c) Of what benefit is free time unless you enjoy the way you use it?

7. fractious
(a) The ice made ominous groaning sounds as we made our way across the pond.
(b) The crew threatened to mutiny unless conditions aboard ship improved.
(c) Four quarters or two halves make one whole.

8. polemic

(a) The skier flew down the hill with her arms outstretched.

(b) The umpire upset the crowd when he threw the shortstop out of the game.

(c) She was unable to give me one good reason why I should change my mind.

9. fulmination

(a) "How dare they set foot on my land after being warned to keep off!"

(b) "With just a little extra effort you can do it; I know you can!"

(c) "Be careful!"

10. filial

(a) Rosemary and her sister were inseparable.

(b) Josiah usually called his parents each week to see how they were.

(c) She ended the letter, "Your loving daughter Catherine."

11E Narrative

Read the narrative below; then complete the exercise that follows it.

WOMEN'S DAY

That crucial 36. In the summer of 1920, only Tennessee could produce the number that would mean victory for suffragists and their supporters. After failed attempts in 1878 and 1914, and after **fulminations** such as the prediction by the senator of Oregon that giving women the right to vote would "make every home a hell on earth," the United States Congress in 1918 passed the Nineteenth Amendment to the Constitution. Thirty-five states had ratified it, and now the issue was before the Tennessee legislature.

A *yes* vote in Tennessee would make female suffrage the law of the land; a tie or a *no* vote would almost certainly render the already passed ratifications **nugatory** since most of the remaining states were opposed to giving women the vote. Furthermore, a negative response from Tennessee would likely erode support in the few states that were wavering. For several weeks prior to the session, tension gripped the capital. National suffragist figures such as Carrie Chapman Catt arrived to advance the women's cause. The factions waged what became known as "The War of the Roses," a reference to the yellow roses worn by supporters of female suffrage and the red ones worn by their opponents. The Tennessee legislature itself was evenly divided, and its members became increasingly **fractious**, pressured not only by vocal **polemicists** but also by the stifling southern summer heat.

On August 18 hundreds of diverse women in big, floppy hats and ankle-length skirts braved the **obloquy** of the men crowded into the corridors and the public gallery of the chamber for the roll call. Among the legislators, Harry Burn, a 24-year-old freshman, felt particular stress. His personal philosophy collided with political reality. Although he believed in a woman's right to vote, he sported a red rose in his lapel. He knew that to do otherwise would jeopardize his chances of being reelected. Struggling with this inner conflict, he twice voted to defer the matter until after the November election. Such **temporizing**, however, only resulted in two 48-48 ties, which kept the issue before the legislature.

The tension in the chamber was **palpable** as the roll call began. With the suffragists in spirit was Febb Ensminger Burn, the mother of Harry Burn. She was unable to be there in person because she was home attending the family farm. When Harry Burn's name was called, a hush came over the chamber. Then came his response: "Aye!" A **cacophony** of mingled cries of shock and joy, cheers and jeers, applause and hisses erupted, for the result was now apparent. When later discussing his surprise move, Mr. Burn explained that just before voting he **perused** a letter recently sent by his mother, a woman appalled at her denial of legal **parity** with men, who could vote on issues affecting her land while she could not. Her message read in part, "Dear Son, Hurrah and vote for suffrage! Don't keep them in doubt. I notice some of the speeches against. They were bitter. I have been watching you to see how you stood but have not noticed anything yet. Don't forget to be a good boy and help Mrs. Catt put the "rat" in ratification. Signed, Your Mother." In a display of **filial** respect, Burn said, "I knew that a mother's advice is always safest for her boy to follow." He also acknowledged that he believed in full suffrage and "appreciated the fact that an opportunity such as this seldom comes to a mortal man."

As the Secretary of State certified the Nineteenth Amendment to the Constitution at a private **convocation** to which no women were invited, he said, in a forced attempt at **jocularity**, "I say to the women of America, you may fire when ready," a reference to the predictions of the political upheaval that increasing the electorate would bring. However, the republic did not fall. What rose was women's rights, sought as long ago as 1776 in Abigail Adams's **supplication** to her husband John when the future second president was in Philadelphia with his **confreres**, attending the birth of the nation. She had written: "In the new code of laws, which I suppose it will be necessary for you to make, I desire you would remember the ladies."

As for Harry Burn, his daring vote not only gave him a place in the history books but also cost him nothing politically. In the November elections, the voters of Mouse Creek returned him to the Tennessee legislature for another term.

Answer each of the following questions in a sentence. Whenever a vocabulary word does not appear in the question, try to use one (or a form of one) in your answer. In a few cases, both question and answer may contain vocabulary words.

1. Give an example from the narrative of the **polemics** vocalized in the United States Senate.

    _____

2. Why is it clear that a majority of the Oregon senator's **confreres** disagreed with him?

    _____

3. How does the narrative show that the tempers of Tennessee legislators were getting short?

    _____

4. Explain why **temporizer** would be a misnomer for Harry Burn's mother.

    _____

5. In what way did Harry Burn's constituents contribute to his inner conflict?

    _____

6. What would have been the result of Tennessee's failure to ratify the Nineteenth Amendment?

    _____

7. Apart from following his mother's directions to vote for suffrage, what evidence is there that Harry Burn highly respected his mother's thinking?

    _____

8. To what emotion did Mrs. Burn appeal in her **supplication** to her son?

    _____

9. What effect did Harry Burn's vote have on the opponents of female suffrage?

    _____

10. How does the narrative convey the atmosphere in the Tennessee legislature as the crucial vote was taken?

    _____

11. What phrase in the narrative provides sound imagery for the moments after Burn's vote is cast?

    _____

12. How did the legislators express their anger at the outcome of the vote?

_____

13. What feigned attitude is expressed in the phrase: "I say to the women of America, you may fire when ready"?

_____

WORDLY WISE

Fulminate is formed from the Latin verb *fulminare,* which means "to strike with lightning." When Jupiter, the king of the Roman gods, *fulminated*, he did so by hurling lightning bolts at whoever had incurred his displeasure. Persons in the modern world who *fulminate* must restrict themselves to hurling verbal abuse or threats.

Fulminate of mercury is a modern and a more literal application of the term; it is a chemical mixture which, under the right conditions, explodes with a flash similar to that of a bolt of lightning.

Lesson 12

Word List
Study the definitions of the words below; then do the exercises for the lesson.

apprise
ə prīz´

v. To make aware of; to inform.
[Marcia *apprised* her employer of her intention of leaving at the end of the year.]

beatific
bē ə ti´ fik

adj. Marked by a joyful appearance; blissful.
[The *beatific* expression of a child at play is captured in this series of photographs.]

cogent
kō´ jənt

adj. Forceful, to the point, and convincing.
[The reporter's *cogent* argument convinced the editor to give her the assignment.]

colloquy
kä´ lə kwe

n. A conversation or dialogue, especially on a serious subject.
[When our *colloquy* became contentious, we decided it was time we took a break.]

deprave
di prāvd´

v. To corrupt morally; to debase.
[Absolute power so *depraved* the Roman emperor Caligula that he committed unimaginable cruelties.]
depravity *n.*

discrete
di skrēt´

adj. Unconnected to other parts; separate and distinct.
[Sand is comprised of tiny, *discrete* particles of rock.]

efface
i fās´

v. **1.** To remove clear evidence of; to rub out or erase.
[The weather over time had partially *effaced* the mural.]
2. To make (oneself) inconspicuous.
[One actor expected the other actors to *efface* themselves so that he could be the star of the show.]

elucidate
i lōō´ sə dāt

v. To make clear by explanation; to clarify.
[The professor *elucidated* Bohr's theory so well that the structure of the atom became quite clear to the class.]

inferno
in fər´ nō

n. Hell or a fiery place that seems like hell; a place of destruction or great suffering.
[Within minutes of the fire starting, the factory was a raging *inferno*.]
infernal *adj.*

lachrymose
la´ krə mōs

adj. Tearful; tending to induce tears; melancholic.
[The *lachrymose* tone of the novel caused me to read only the first chapter.]

morbid
môr´ bəd

adj. **1.** Marked by gloomy or unwholesome thoughts.
[My grandmother's daily reading of the obituary page indicated not *morbid* curiosity, but concern for her neighbors.]
2. Affected by or caused by disease.
[Removing the *morbid* tissue from his liver cured the patient.]

omniscient äm ni´ shənt	*adj.* Aware of everything that is going on; all-knowing. [Professor Wu doesn't pretend to be *omniscient,* but she knows a great deal about almost every subject.] **omniscience** *n.*
palliative pa´ lē ā tiv	*adj.* Serving to make less painful or severe. [The hospice program delivers *palliative* services to those who are gravely ill.] **palliative** *n.*
preternatural prē tər na´ chə rəl	*adj.* Beyond what is normal or natural; incapable of being explained or understood. [Either he possesses *preternatural* power that enables him to bend spoons without touching them, or he is a charlatan.]
salutary sal´ yə ter ē	*adj.* **1.** Promoting a beneficial effect. [The idea of losing telephone privileges had a *salutary* effect on Kit's doing her homework.] **2.** Healthful. [Wearing sunblock will have a *salutary* effect on your skin.]

12A Understanding Meanings

Read the sentences in each group below. If a sentence correctly uses the word in boldface, write C on the line of the corresponding number below the group. If a sentence is incorrect, rewrite it so that the vocabulary word in boldface is used correctly.

■   1. An **inferno** is a fiery place or state of great destruction and suffering.
2. A **salutary** treatment is one that is welcoming.
3. To **efface** oneself is to try to stay in the background.
4. A **palliative** is something that eases pain or distress.
5. A **depraved** person is one who lacks the basic necessities of life.

1. _____

2. _____

3. _____

4. _____

5. _____

■ 6. To be **morbid** is to be subject to death.
    7. To **elucidate** a plan is to explain it fully and carefully.
    8. A **beatific** expression is one that is full of joy.
    9. **Omniscience** is the study of life in all its forms.
    10. A **colloquy** is a light meal or snack.

    6. _____

    7. _____

    8. _____

    9. _____

    10. _____

■ 11. A **discrete** part is one that is separate from those around it.
    12. A **preternatural** occurrence is one that goes beyond the ordinary.
    13. To **apprise** someone is to make a judgment concerning that person.
    14. **Cogent** testimony is persuasive and to the point.
    15. A **lachrymose** goodbye is one during which tears are shed.

    11. _____

    12. _____

    13. _____

    14. _____

    15. _____

12B Using Words

If the word (or a form of the word) in boldface fits in a sentence in the group below it, write the word in the blank space. If the word does not fit, leave the space empty.

1. **colloquy**
   (a) The _____ was called to resolve a number of outstanding issues.
   (b) My _____ was in the form of a private letter addressed to the bishop.
   (c) "Shmooze" is a _____ for "engage in casual conversation."

2. **morbid**
   (a) A preoccupation with crimes of violence could be described as _____ .
   (b) All humans must face the fact that they are _____ .
   (c) The lab tests show no signs of _____ tissue in the patient's pancreas.

3. **deprave**
   (a) Many people will argue that violent movies tend to _____ young minds.
   (b) These comical scenes could only have been written by a _____ individual.
   (c) People who are _____ of nutritional food cannot function at their fullest potential.

4. **apprised**
   (a) Was he _____ of the fact that he was required to attend the meeting?
   (b) The small house was _____ at ninety-nine thousand dollars.
   (c) Had Leah been _____ of the situation, she would have acted differently.

5. **palliative**
   (a) Calamine lotion has a _____ effect on poison ivy.
   (b) The puppies looked so _____ that I was concerned for their health.
   (c) This new drug is merely a _____ and is not claimed to be a cure.

6. **beatific**
   (a) A _____ smile lit up the face of the child who played the part of Tiny Tim.
   (b) We found a _____ spot by the river and set up our camp there.
   (c) The food at the gourmet buffet was absolutely _____ .

7. **preternatural**
   (a) Some _____ force unknown to physics powered these strange crafts.
   (b) I was unnerved by her _____ ability to know what I was thinking.
   (c) Countess Zamboni's _____ mental powers enable her to perform amazing feats.

8. **cogent**
   (a) The article gives a _____ analysis of the state of the economy.
   (b) The speaker delivered some _____ criticism about the current nonfiction best-seller.
   (c) This matter is so _____ that it must receive the highest priority.

12C Synonyms, Antonyms, Analogies

Each group of four words below contains two words that are either synonyms or antonyms. Circle these two words; then circle the S if they are synonyms, the A if they are antonyms.

1. PRETERNATURAL   VIVIPAROUS
   EXTRAORDINARY   LACHRYMOSE   S   A

2. APPRISE   CONVOKE
   ENRAGE   ELUCIDATE   S   A

3. HELLISH   INFERNAL
   OMNISCIENT   PALPABLE   S   A

4. AGGRAVATING   MORBID
   PALLIATIVE   APPOSITE   S   A

5. COGENT   DISCRETE
   GLOOMY   SEPARATE   S   A

Complete the analogies by selecting the pair of words whose relationship most resembles the relationship of the pair in capital letters. Circle the letter in front of the pair you choose.

6. SALUBRIOUS : SALUTARY ::
   (a) torpid : fractious   (c) helpful : beneficent
   (b) earnest : vacuous   (d) benighted : dark

7. LACHRYMOSE : TEARS ::
   (a) sedulous : tasks   (c) prodigal : gifts
   (b) internecine : wars   (d) risible : laughs

8. WISE : OMNISCIENT ::
   (a) optimistic : utopian   (c) fecund : sterile
   (b) sociable : egregious   (d) arrogant : proud

9. MOOD : MORBID ::
   (a) idea : cogent   (c) disease : depressing
   (b) scent : beneficent   (d) thought : banal

10. COUPLE : BEATIFIC ::
   (a) pair : convivial
   (b) rulers : autocratic
   (c) people : bereft
   (d) tyrants : beneficent

12D Images of Words

Circle the letter of each sentence that suggests the numbered boldface vocabulary word. In each group, you may circle more than one letter or none at all.

1. **apprise**
(a) Winners of the competition will be notified by mail.
(b) The dealer told Serena that her car was worth two thousand dollars.
(c) I shared the contents of the letter with my friend Aimee.

2. **omniscient**
(a) They believe in a higher power who knows all things.
(b) Dr. Gonzalez is fluent in seven languages.
(c) Animal rights activists believe that all experimentation on animals should end.

3. **salutary**
(a) The best thing Marge could do for her health would be to stop drinking.
(b) The marchers raised their hats as they passed the reviewing stand.
(c) Al felt better after I had a long, encouraging talk with him.

4. **inferno**
(a) Internecine fighting in the city caused many explosions that injured innocent citizens.
(b) Jonathan Edwards' powerful sermon "Sinners in the Hands of an Angry God" is often included in collections of Puritan literature.
(c) The heat was so intense that even firefighters could not immediately enter the building.

5. **efface**
(a) The teacher put a sticker with a smiling face on her student's paper.
(b) Stephano was not one to draw attention to himself.
(c) The clearing showed no signs of campers ever having been there.

6. **cogent**
(a) Urmila's hand shot up every time the teacher asked a question.
(b) I sent the letter by overnight delivery to be sure it would arrive promptly.
(c) The directions for assembling the swing set made no sense to me.

7. **lachrymose**
(a) The comedian had me laughing until the tears rolled down my face.
(b) I wept openly at the end of the play when the kind, gentle old man dies.
(c) When you're feeling down, it's good to remember that moods come and go.

8. **colloquy**

(a) A modern term for a group of experts organized for interdisciplinary research is *think tank*.
(b) The plane was in radio contact with the ground throughout the flight.
(c) We served a simple lunch of soup, crusty bread, and fruit.

9. **elucidate**

(a) The searchlight picked out the climber halfway up the rocky face of the mountain.
(b) Footnotes help the reader to understand the more difficult passages.
(c) The union leader explained the terms of the new contract to the members before they voted on ratifying it.

10. **discrete**

(a) I know that I can trust my friend Emily to keep a secret.
(b) Gases are made up of molecules jostling against each other.
(c) Pointillist paintings are made by applying tiny dots of paint to the canvas.

12E Narrative

Read the narrative below; then complete the exercise that follows it.

ON DEATH AND DYING

Death and Dying? Frightening words? They needn't be, according to Swiss-born psychiatrist Elizabeth Kubler-Ross. To her, there is nothing **morbid** about the subject when the experience includes support, compassion, love, and **palliative** care. In fact, she sees dying as the final stage of human growth. What may appear at first to be a radical position is actually a peaceful stance arrived at after many experiences confronting death in its cruelest forms.

Elizabeth Kubler-Ross was thirteen in 1939 when Nazi Germany plunged Europe into the **inferno** of the Second World War. In its aftermath, as a volunteer in the International Voluntary Service for Peace, she helped survivors rebuild their lives in Poland. Here she came face to face with the full extent of Nazi **depravity** when she visited Majdanek concentration camp. The mountain of little shoes left by the children before they were herded into the gas chambers and the drawings of butterflies that they had scratched on the walls of the huts were sights she could never **efface** from her memory. At the age of nineteen, Kubler-Ross witnessed death in a **preternatural** form.

After returning to Switzerland and graduating from medical school, Dr. Kubler-Ross came to New York in 1958 on a fellowship in psychiatry. In the United States, she found that terminally ill patients were kept in hospitals where they were often fed through tubes, attached to life-support systems, stripped of all dignity, and enduring great pain. Often assuming an air of **omniscience**, many physicians never considered that a patient might prefer to be left alone to die in peace as comfortably as possible. Death was the enemy; the loss of a patient was a major defeat. It had to be fought every step of the way.

The American way of death was exceedingly different from what Kubler-Ross had known as a family physician in Switzerland. There, she attended terminally ill patients in their own homes. Far from **lachrymose**, death scenes on these occasions were marked by a quiet dignity and calm acceptance on the part of both the dying person and the family members.

While at the University of Chicago in the late 1960s, Dr. Kubler-Ross sought to change the American attitude toward death. She held a series of **colloquies** with terminally ill cancer patients before groups of medical students and members of the clergy. From these encounters she was able to observe, and later **elucidate**, the complexity of people's reactions when they realize they have only a short time to live. She identified five **discrete** stages. First comes denial: "This can't be happening to me." Next comes anger: "Why me? What have I done to deserve this?" Then comes bargaining, either with God or oneself: "Let me stay alive until my daughter's wedding, and I'll never get angry with my children again." The fourth stage is depression: "I can't be bothered to take care of my appearance. Nothing matters any more." Finally comes acceptance: "I would never have believed that I could find the strength to face this so calmly."

In 1969 Dr. Kubler-Ross **cogently** expressed these ideas in her book *On Death and Dying,* which quickly became a bestseller. Although many professionals argue that Dr. Kubler-Ross's model oversimplifies the dimensions of dying, its effect on the American medical profession's treatment of the terminally ill was both dramatic and **salutary**. It led to the formation in the United States of the first hospices, facilities that attend to the physical, emotional, and spiritual needs of the dying and their families. Such was Dr. Kubler-Ross's promotion of the movement, including her convincing lectures and workshops, that by the mid-1990s there were over two thousand hospices in the United States.

Now nearing the end of her life and disabled by a series of paralyzing strokes, Elizabeth Kubler-Ross, **apprised** of her own situation, maintains her position. In a 1995 interview, when she was asked how she herself feels about dying, a **beatific** peacefulness entered her eyes. "It's just the most beautiful thing that can ever happen to you," she replied. And reflecting on her visit as a nineteen-year-old to the Nazi death camp in Poland, she had this to say: "I would never have gone into the work on death and dying without Majdanek. All the hospices came out of that concentration camp."

Answer each of the following questions in a sentence. Whenever a vocabulary word does not appear in the question, try to use one (or a form of one) in your answer. In a few cases, both question and answer may contain vocabulary words.

1. Who in the narrative is best exemplified by the word *depraved*?

   _____

2. How do you know that the Nazi's **preternatural** acts made an indelible impression on Elizabeth Kubler-Ross?

   _____

3. Was Elizabeth Kubler-Ross's contemplation of her own death **lachrymose**? Explain your answer.

   _____

4. In what way did doctors in the United States act differently from doctors in Europe?

   _____

5. How were the Chicago cancer patients able to **elucidate** their feelings to Kubler-Ross?

   _____

6. Why is the word *discrete* applicable to Kubler-Ross's model of the dimensions of dying?

   _____

7. How does Kubler-Ross's book demonstrate her sharp **cognitive** skills?

   _____

8. What effect did Kubler-Ross's book have on the practice of medicine in the United States?

   _____

9. Why is **palliative** care the only treatment for the terminally ill?

   _____

10. How did Kubler-Ross demonstrate that she does not regard her own death as a **morbid** subject?

    _____

WORDLY WISE

To be *discreet* is to show prudence and self-restraint in what one says or does. To be **discrete** is to consist of separate and distinct parts. Although these two words have quite different meanings, they share a common root. Both are derived from the Latin *discernere*, "to separate" or "to perceive differences." Note that a discreet person perceives the difference between what may be said or done and what may not.

The Latin for *light* is *lux*, and several English words share this root. A *translucent* material is one through which light can pass. A *lucent* object is one that gives off light. A *lucid* explanation is one that makes clear what previously was hidden. A *lucifer* is an early type of friction match. And to **elucidate** a subject is to shed light upon it by explaining it.

The Latin prefix *omni-* means "all" and is found in several English words. *Bus* is a shortened form of *omnibus*, which is a Latin word meaning "for all." An *omnibus* was not a private vehicle, but was available for all who wished to use it. An *omnivorous* animal is one that eats all kinds of food. An *omnipotent* being is one who is all-powerful. Something that is *omnipresent* is present everywhere. And to be **omniscient** is to be all-knowing.

Crossword Puzzle

Solve the crossword puzzle below by studying the clues and filling in the answer boxes. Clues followed by a number are definitions of words in lessons 9 through 12. The number gives the word list from which the answer to the clue is taken.

Clues Across

1. Argument to refute another's opinions (11)
4. Easy to touch, see, or feel (11)
9. Forcefully and convincingly expressed (12)
10. Given to or characterized by joking (11)
12. An activity at which a person excels (10)
13. Having a saw-toothed edge (9)
16. Wastefully extravagant (10)
20. All-knowing (12)
21. One with fine taste in food and drink (9)
24. An island in the Mediterranean Sea
25. To act evasively to gain time (11)
27. The Congressional _____ of Honor
28. To clear from alleged guilt (9)
29. To summon; to call or bring together (11)

Clues Down

1. To read or examine closely (11)
2. Tearful or inducing tears (12)
3. Boat that is paddled
5. Relevant; apt (9)
6. Turned or twisted to one side (10)
7. All the graduates of a college
8. Of, on, or near the back (9)
11. Capital of Norway
14. Separate and distinct (12)
15. Of, at, from, or towards the side (9)
17. A statement or pronouncement (10)
18. A fiery place (12)
19. Meal eaten outdoors
22. Abundance
23. To remove clear evidence of (12)
26. Used in hockey

Lesson 13

Word List

Study the definitions of the words below; then do the exercises for the lesson.

abut
ə but´

v. To be next to; to border on.
[Because your neighbor's property *abuts* yours, she must give her approval before you make these structural changes.]

adjure
ə joor´

v. **1.** To command solemnly.
[The judge *adjured* the jurors to examine the evidence very carefully.]
2. To advise sincerely.
[The guidance counselor *adjured* the student to submit his original essay as part of his college application.]

descry
di skrī´

v. To catch sight of a distant object after looking carefully.
[With a telescope he constructed in 1609, Galileo was able to *descry* Saturn's rings.]

desecrate
de´ si krāt

v. To misuse or violate something sacred.
[Graffiti on the steps of the cathedral *desecrated* the old building.]
desecration *n.*

dilettante
di´ lə tänt

n. A person with only a superficial interest and slight knowledge of an art or other field of knowledge.
[She claims to be only a *dilettante* at writing poetry, but actually her work is quite good.]

equivocal
i kwi´ və kəl

adj. **1.** Having more than one meaning or interpretation, usually intended to confuse.
["I usually eat alone," was Amitar's *equivocal* answer when asked if anyone had accompanied him to the restaurant.]
2. Uncertain or undecided.
[The candidate's *equivocal* position on the issue rankled both sides.]
equivocate *v.* To speak in a way that deliberately obscures one's position.

exhume
ig zoom´

v. **1.** To dig out of the ground.
[Early in the twentieth century, archeologists *exhumed* artifacts from a pharaoh's tomb constructed around 1300 B.C.]
2. To recover from neglect; to revive.
[The band *exhumed* some old English music hall songs and delighted modern audiences with them.]

extirpate
ek´ stər pāt

v. To destroy completely; to wipe out.
[Whole species unknown to us are *extirpated* by the destruction of the world's rain forests.]

foible
foi´ bəl

n. A small fault or weakness in a person's character.
[Ava's occasional short temper was a mere *foible* compared to her ongoing magnanimous spirit.]

insolvent
in säl´ vənt

adj. Without the means to pay what is owed; bankrupt.
[His age was the ostensible reason for his retiring, but the truth is his company is now *insolvent*.]

| **jocose** | *adj.* Given to joking; humorous and playful. |
| jō kōs´ | [Ms. Langton's *jocose* manner in the classroon did not impede her skillful teaching.] |

| **portal** | *n.* A door or entrance, especially one that is large and imposing. |
| pōr´ tl | [The *portal* of the Boston Public Library was carved by Daniel Chester French.] |

| **progenitor** | *n.* A direct ancestor. |
| prō je´ nə tər | [The Anasazi people were the *progenitors* of the Hopi Native Americans.] |

| **propitiate** | *v.* To overcome distrust or hostility; to appease. |
| prō pi´ shē āt | [The Aztecs believed that the way to *propitiate* their gods was with human sacrifices.] |

| **restitution** | *n.* A paying back for what has been lost or damaged. |
| res tə tōō´ shən | [The investors in the failed enterprise made sedulous efforts to obtain *restitution* from its organizers.] |

13A Understanding Meanings

Read the sentences in each group below. If a sentence correctly uses the word in boldface, write C on the line of the corresponding number below the group. If a sentence is incorrect, rewrite it so that the vocabulary word in boldface is used correctly.

■ 1. A **jocose** person is one who likes to amuse people by making jokes.
   2. A **foible** is a short story that has a moral.
   3. A business that is **insolvent** has debts that it cannot pay.
   4. A **progenitor** is a person from whom someone is descended.
   5. To **exhume** something is to suppose that it is a fact.

1. _____

2. _____

3. _____

4. _____

5. _____

■ 6. To **extirpate** something is to hasten it along.
   7. Housing lots that **abut** share a common boundary line.
   8. To **desecrate** a monument is to treat it irreverently.
   9. **Restitution** is the making up for some injury.
  10. A **dilettante** is a young woman making her entrance into society.

6. _____

7. _____

8. _____

9. _____

10. _____

■ 11. To **descry** something is to speak out forcefully against it.

12. An **equivocal** statement is one that can be taken either of two ways.

13. To **propitiate** someone is to win that person's goodwill.

14. To **adjure** someone is to give them permission to leave.

15. A **portal** is a small opening in the side of a ship to admit light.

11. _____

12. _____

13. _____

14. _____

15. _____

13B Using Words

If the word (or a form of the word) in boldface fits in a sentence in the group below it, write the word in the blank space. If the word does not fit, leave the space empty.

1. **portal**
   (a) A swinging _____ cut into the door allowed the cats to come and go freely.
   (b) The _____ to the temple was flanked on either side by carved stone lions.
   (c) Plane passengers are requested to exit by way of the rear _____ .

2. **exhume**
   (a) Relatives plan to _____ the poet's remains for burial in her native Italy.
   (b) We cannot _____ that the other groups will join our coalition.
   (c) Fido loves to _____ the bones he has buried in the garden.

3. **abut**
   (a) All of the houses on this street _____ Long Pond.
   (b) In the community garden, one person's plot for planting _____ another's.
   (c) The names Adams and Adamson _____ each other in the class register.

4. **restitution**
    (a) I offered to make _____ for the damage I had accidentally done to the patio.
    (b) The _____ of Charles II to the English throne occurred in 1660.
    (c) We offered a substantial _____ to the person finding our lost dog.

5. **extirpate**
    (a) Please _____ the word "Anaconda" and replace it with "Anconia."
    (b) The Romans destroyed the city of Carthage and _____ its citizens.
    (c) The French revolutionaries were determined to _____ the nobility.

6. **propitiate**
    (a) This seemed a _____ time to bring up the subject of a raise in my summer job.
    (b) Hazel successfully _____ Todd by apologizing for speaking so intemperately to him.
    (c) Baking soda and water will _____ your upset stomach.

7. **descry**
    (a) I could _____ no interest in renting that video.
    (b) As the ship drew near the island, the crew could _____ no sign of life.
    (c) I could _____ the sound of laughter from somewhere in the building.

8. **adjure**
    (a) The work was hard, but we soon became _____ to it.
    (b) When you take the oath, you are _____ to speak the truth.
    (c) As they were about to leave the courtroom, the judge _____ the lawyers to refrain from commenting on the case.

13C Synonyms, Antonyms, Analogies

Each group of four words below contains two words that are either synonyms or antonyms. Circle these two words; then circle the S if they are synonyms, the A if they are antonyms.

1. EXTIRPATE   BURY
    EXHUME   EXCULPATE   S   A

2. PROTAGONIST   ANCESTOR
    PROGENITOR   DILETTANTE   S   A

3. IRRITATE   PROPITIATE
   DESECRATE   EXTIRPATE   S   A

4. DESCRY   COMMAND
   ADJURE   ABUT   S   A

5. RESTITUTION VIOLATION
   ACCESS   DESECRATION   S   A

Complete the analogies by selecting the pair of words whose relationship most resembles the relationship of the pair in capital letters. Circle the letter in front of the pair you choose.

6. DILETTANTE : SAVANT ::
   (a) ascetic : epicure
   (b) apathy : élan
   (c) interloper : aborigine
   (d) amateur : professional

7. INSOLVENT : CASH ::
   (a) risible : laughter
   (b) torpid : energy
   (c) veritable : truth
   (d) fecund : children

8. DOOR : PORTAL ::
   (a) village : town
   (b) moat : castle
   (c) house : residence
   (d) glass : window

9. JOCOSE : HILARIOUS ::
   (a) apathetic : indifferent
   (b) weak : feeble
   (c) brave : intrepid
   (d) ardent : altruistic

10. EQUIVOCAL : OPINIONATED ::
    (a) parsimonious : generous
    (b) exalted : exemplary
    (c) tenacious : stubborn
    (d) prodigal : indigent

13D Images of Words

Circle the letter of each sentence that suggests the numbered boldface vocabulary word. In each group, you may circle more than one letter or none at all.

1. **dilettante**
   (a) Freddie tends to dawdle, so he is frequently late.
   (b) My date for the prom looked so attractive in his tuxedo.
   (c) The carpentry workshop is not intended for skilled practitioners of the craft.

2. descry

(a) Looking at the photographs of the famine victims was very upsetting.

(b) The two reds were similar, but one was slightly paler than the other.

(c) The crowd began to cheer when the first sail came into view.

3. progenitor

(a) According to the Bible, the human race is descended from Adam and Eve.

(b) Queen Victoria is the great-great-grandmother of Queen Elizabeth II.

(c) According to evolutionary theory, humans and apes share a common ancestor.

4. insolvent

(a) These salts remain in suspension and will not dissolve in water.

(b) The management admitted that the company was unable to pay its debts.

(c) Even Sherlock Holmes would be unable to solve this mystery!

5. equivocal

(a) I might go, but, on the other hand, my friends think I should stay.

(b) Jules paused for a minute and then replied, "Well, yes and no."

(c) At that time the dollar was worth about twelve pesos.

6. restitution

(a) The picture was slightly damaged in the flood but was easily repaired.

(b) Ms. Sahakian made a generous contribution to a fund that helped homeless people.

(c) At this point, the family is totally out of money.

7. abut

(a) The island is joined to the mainland by a mile-long bridge.

(b) This piece of property is right on the town line.

(c) In the dance, the partners extended their hands until they touched.

8. desecrate

(a) Vandals had overturned tombstones in the graveyard.

(b) The police caught the person who slashed the tires on my car.

(c) The citizens were horrified at the idea of building a mall on the site of the Civil War battlefield.

9. jocose

(a) Uncle Andy could find the humor in any situation.

(b) I found it difficult not to laugh at my own error.

(c) The Ruiz family agreed that their trip to Disneyland was fantastic.

10. foible

(a) I was so excited about trying this recipe, but the actual experience turned into a disaster.

(b) I don't know whether to believe her, because she sometimes stretches the truth.

(c) A weak ankle prevented Nazneen from taking part in gymnastics.

13E Narrative

Read the narrative below; then complete the exercise that follows it.

MENDING THE BROKEN CIRCLE

When the Smithsonian's National Museum of the American Indian (NMAI) opened its New York base in October 1994, it began a new chapter in the long and troubled history of relations between Native Americans and Americans of European descent. The site in lower Manhattan was aptly chosen, for it was from near that spot in 1624 that members of the Lenape Nation **descried** the Dutch ships bringing the first white settlers to their shores. Now, centuries later, the **portals** of the old Custom House (now the NMAI) lead to exhibitions and educational programs reflecting the diversity of Native-American peoples.

Linda Poolaw, who was the Grand Chief of the Delaware Nation when the museum opened, counts the Lenape among her **progenitors**. She helped to choose many of the works of art housed there and describes its opening as representing the partial reconnection of a circle that was broken. John Colonghi, the museum's main fundraiser, recalls his Eskimo mother telling him that as a child going to school on an Alaskan island she was beaten if she spoke her native language. He sees the NMAI as an attempt to make partial **restitution** for white America's efforts to **extirpate** Native-American culture.

The New York museum is named the George Gustave Heye Center in honor of the man who made the NMAI possible. Collecting Native-American objects became an obsession with this wealthy banker, and for over fifty years, until his death in 1957, he scoured the Americas from the Arctic Circle to Tierra Del Fuego. A member of the New England Abenaki tribe once remarked **jocosely** after a visit from Heye, "We were lucky to be left with our underwear."

When he died in 1957, Heye had accumulated over one million objects ranging from artifacts like weathered clothing and blankets to art objects such as masks, stone and wood carvings, and gold work. Despite his long exposure to them, Heye's involvement with Native-American cultures was never more than that of a **dilettante** who liked collecting things.

Stored in a warehouse in the Bronx, this vast treasury gathered dust until the early 1980s when the foundation Heye had established to oversee it became **insolvent**, and the trustees turned the entire collection over to the Smithsonian. Lynne Harlan, the NMAI collection manager and a Qualla Boundary Cherokee from North Carolina, was rummaging through boxes at the Bronx warehouse when she **exhumed** six Qualla masks together with bones that could have belonged to her ancestors. Harlan was offended by the act of **desecration** that had brought their remains to the Bronx and wanted to **propitiate** the wounded spirits she feels inhabit the warehouse. She offers daily prayers to them. In accordance with tribal ritual, she lights a smudge pot to carry her prayers to the sky with the smoke.

When the NMAI was established by a 1989 Act of Congress as the fifteenth of the Smithsonian Institute's member museums, clear policies were mandated. For one, the Act **adjured** the museum to return all human remains to the tribes from whom they were taken, together with sacred and ceremonial objects necessary for the revitalization of Native-American religions. This task was the responsibility of Clara Sue Kidwell, who is an Oklahoma Choctaw. Its completion marked yet another partial reconnection of a circle that was broken. Additionally, the Act required that two-thirds of the NMAI's senior managers be Native American. It also specified that the last vacant spot, **abutting** the National Air and Space Museum on the Mall in Washington, D.C., be set aside as a second site for the NMAI; at a third location in Maryland, a resource center will store the bulk of the museum's art and cultural objects.

NMAI director Richard West, a member of the Cheyenne and Arapoho tribes of Oklahoma, is **equivocal** about Mr. Heye. On the one hand, he took from Native Americans much of their heritage to satisfy what was no more than a rich man's **foible.** On the other hand, had he not pursued his quest so relentlessly, such a museum, holding four million catalogued items and 10,000 years of Native-American heritage, might not exist today.

Answer each of the following questions in a sentence. Whenever a vocabulary word does not appear in the question, try to use one (or a form of one) in your answer. In a few cases, both question and answer may contain vocabulary words.

1. Give one likely reason for congress's funding of the NMAI.

   _____

2. Linda Poolaw helped select art objects for the museum's New York site. Why was she an appropriate person for this role?

   _____

3. Where did Congress locate the Washington branch of the NMAI?

   _____

4. What architectural feature of the New York museum lends a stately air to the site?

   _____

5. Give evidence that Heye knew little of the history of the objects he collected.

   _____

6. What led the Heye foundation to donate the collection to the Smithsonian?

_____

7. What was Lynne Harlan's reaction when she **exhumed** ancient bones and six Qualla masks from the warehouse storage boxes?

_____

8. In what way did John Colonghi's mother experience disrespect for her culture?

_____

9. What tone is conveyed in the remark "We were lucky to be left with our underwear"?

_____

WORDLY WISE

Don't confuse **descry** with _decry_ (Lesson 8). To **descry** is to spy out or discover with the eye; to decry something is to disparage it. Curiously, both words are derived from the Old French verb _descrier_, "to cry out" or "cry down" (decry).

A person giving an **equivocal** response to a question requiring a _yes_ or _no_ answer could be said to be speaking with two voices, equally strong, one saying "yes" and the other saying "no." This is suggested by the origin of the word. It is formed from the Latin _equi,-_ meaning "equal," or "even," and _vox_, meaning "voice."

Lesson 14

Word List

Study the definitions of the words below; then do the exercises for the lesson.

acerbic
ə sur´ bik

adj. **1.** Bitter or sour to the taste.
[Cranberries are *acerbic* and require sweetening to make them palatable.]
2. Biting or stinging in tone; sarcastic.
[The comic's *acerbic* humor made her victims squirm even as they laughed.]

canard
kə närd´

n. A groundless report or story, often one made up deliberately to deceive.
[The newspaper story that claimed the athlete was distracted by problems at home was actually a *canard* concocted by her competitors.]

debonair
de bə nar´

adj. Elegant in appearance and charming in manner.
[*Debonair* and urbane, the British-born American-film actor Cary Grant is one of the best-known leading men of all time.]

deign
dān

v. To lower oneself in one's own estimation; to condescend.
[In his drama *Pygmalion*, George Bernard Shaw creates a character "of class" who *deigns* to interact with one beneath his social status.]

dotage
dō´ tij

n. Mental deterioration associated with advanced age.
[King Lear was in his *dotage* when he foolishly decided to divide his kingdom among his daughters.]

foist
foist

v. To impose something unwanted or unneeded on an unwilling recipient.
[My friend, with good intentions, tried to *foist* some of her old clothes on me when she was cleaning out her closet.]

insipid
in si´ pəd

adj. **1.** Tasteless.
[Oscar insisted that a recipe without a dash of Tabasco sauce would make for *insipid* soup.]
2. Lacking excitement; uninteresting.
[I find most TV sitcoms so *insipid* that I can't bear to watch them.]

misconstrue
mis kən stroo´

v. To misunderstand or misinterpret.
[I'm afraid I *misconstrued* her silence as agreement and went ahead with the project.]

narcissism
när´ sə si zəm

n. Excessive admiration of oneself.
[The writer's *narcissism* was blatant in his repeated use of the word *I* in his memoirs.]
narcissistic *adj.*

overweening
ō vər wē´ niŋ

adj. **1.** Excessively proud.
[She strode onto the stage with an *overweening* attitude that elicited only polite rather than enthusiastic applause.]
2. Lacking restraint; immoderate.
[Ethan Frome's *overweening* insecurity was the flaw that led to his tragic life.]

paean
pē´ ən

n. A hymn of joy, praise, or appreciation.
[Shelley's ode that begins "Hail to thee, blithe spirit" is a *paean* to the skylark.]

132

repartee re pər tē´	*n.* Conversation marked by quick and witty verbal exchanges. [The *repartee* between the rock star and her accompanist had the fans at the concert laughing repeatedly.]
repine ri pīn´	*v.* To express deep sadness or discontent; to long for something lost. [Rather than *repine* over the loss of Checkers, the children found a cat at the animal shelter to take her place.]
sartorial sär tōr´ ē əl	*adj.* Relating to clothing, especially tailored clothing. [Ben's habitual attire of T-shirt and jeans expressed his casual attitude about his *sartorial* appearance.]
svelte svelt	*adj.* Slender and graceful; having sleek lines. [*Svelte* ballerinas played the parts of the swans.]

14A Understanding Meanings

Read the sentences in each group below. If a sentence correctly uses the word in boldface, write C on the line of the corresponding number below the group. If a sentence is incorrect, rewrite it so that the vocabulary word in boldface is used correctly.

■ 1. A **svelte** figure is one that is slim and graceful.
  2. An **acerbic** article is one that boldly protests something.
  3. A **paean** is a worker who performs menial labor.
  4. To **repine** is to be in low spirits.
  5. **Dotage** is a measured amount of something, as a drug or medicine.

1. _____
2. _____
3. _____
4. _____
5. _____

■ 6. An **insipid** conversation is one that lacks sparkle.
  7. To **deign** is to invest someone with authority.
  8. **Repartee** is dialogue consisting of clever retorts in quick succession.
  9. **Sartorial** concerns are those having to do with ethics or morals.
 10. To **foist** things on someone is to thrust them on that person.

6. _____
7. _____
8. _____

9. _____

10. _____

■ 11. A **narcissistic** person is one with an unduly high opinion of himself or herself.
  12. To **misconstrue** an explanation is to mistake the meaning of it.
  13. A **canard** is an expression of joy or appreciation.
  14. An **overweening** appetite is one that eschews moderation.
  15. A **debonair** person is one with many creditors and little money.

11. _____

12. _____

13. _____

14. _____

15. _____

14B Using Words

If the word (or a form of the word) in boldface fits in a sentence in the group below it, write the word in the blank space. If the word does not fit, leave the space empty.

1. **svelte**
   (a) The _____ way they managed to fool us was what made me angry.
   (b) Using only _____ models to advertise clothes can give a false impression of what is attractive and fashionable.
   (c) Seeing the _____ book he lent me told me it wouldn't take long to read.

2. **deign**
   (a) Our organization has no interest in a person whose attitude is "I guess I'll _____ to speak to them."
   (b) The child stared in wonder at the Great _____ .
   (c) Nana did not _____ it necessary to accompany the children on their walk.

3. **repartee**
   (a) The speaker's clever _____ with some of the hecklers in the audience soon put an end to their interruption.
   (b) Alka finished writing her _____ just in time to submit it before the deadline.
   (c) We had developed such a _____ that we could perceive each other's thoughts.

4. **dotage**
   (a) Just because Alberto's memory fails occasionally doesn't mean he's in his _____ .
   (b) When the horses reach their _____ , they are put out to pasture.
   (c) My aunt is looking for some fabric with _____ on it to make a cushion for the stool.

5. **paean**

    (a) The finale of Beethoven's Ninth Symphony is a _____ to the human spirit.

    (b) Sonali's grudging "thank you" was a poor _____ for all I had done for her.

    (c) The song is a _____ expressing the suffering of slaves in the South.

6. **foist**

    (a) The steelworkers _____ the girder high onto the building by using a special crane.

    (b) Unscrupulous brokers _____ worthless stock upon unsuspecting investors.

    (c) Don't let the builder _____ you into paying for repairs you haven't agreed to.

7. **overweening**

    (a) After the long hike, our _____ desire was for a hot shower and a soft bed.

    (b) "I want to be a success, but I don't want to fall victim to _____ ambition."

    (c) Her _____ love of power made her oblivious to those she hurt to get ahead.

8. **misconstrue**

    (a) "You _____ my intention if you thought I meant to offend you."

    (b) The next passage is a difficult one, and students often _____ it.

    (c) The child moved her pencil back and forth to _____ the path leading to the exit of the maze.

14C Synonyms, Antonyms, Analogies

Each group of four words below contains two words that are either synonyms or antonyms. Circle these two words; then circle the S if they are synonyms, the A if they are antonyms.

1. REPINE	SUPPLICATE		
CELEBRATE	MISCONSTRUE	S	A
2. CONVOKE	FOIST		
DEIGN	CONDESCEND	S	A
3. OVERWEENING	SLOVENLY		
DEBONAIR	MAWKISH	S	A
4. NARCISSISTIC	MODEST		
SARTORIAL	FRACTIOUS	S	A

5. INSIPID   SVELTE
   PUNGENT   PRIMEVAL   S   A

Complete the analogies by selecting the pair of words whose relationship most resembles the relationship of the pair in capital letters. Circle the letter in front of the pair you choose.

6. CANARD : TRUTH ::
   (a) polemic : vigor   (c) apothegm : brevity
   (b) wraith : substance   (d) doyen : respect

7. SVELTE : SHAPE ::
   (a) hostile : vendetta   (c) pale : color
   (b) wet : liquid   (d) prescient : knowledge

8. SARTORIAL : CLOTHING ::
   (a) insolvent : business   (c) equivocal : fairness
   (b) pecuniary : money   (d) parochial : education

9. PAEAN : CELEBRATE ::
   (a) lament : mourn   (c) performance : applaud
   (b) credo : believe   (d) invocation : elicit

10. QUICK : REPARTEE ::
    (a) sumptuous : banquet   (c) angry : tirade
    (b) acerbic : taste   (d) extinct : volcano

14D Images of Words

Circle the letter of each sentence that suggests the numbered boldface vocabulary word. In each group, you may circle more than one letter or none at all.

1. insipid
(a) His foolish remarks and braying laughter embarrassed everyone present.
(b) Her prose style makes dull what should have been an exciting account.
(c) The dish would have been improved by the addition of a few spices.

2. debonair
(a) Simon's easy charm and stylish dress made him a popular figure on the stage.
(b) The yacht was a sleek sixty-foot craft in immaculate condition.
(c) We found him lovable despite his gruff manner and rumpled appearance.

3. narcissism

(a) Sharon had arranged photos of herself all around her bedroom.

(b) The most interesting person at the dinner was the actress Dolores del Monte.

(c) He was gazing admiringly at himself in the mirror and scarcely noticed us.

4. canard

(a) We assured Deena that the magician's rabbit had not suddenly appeared out of the air.

(b) There is no truth to the report of a UFO landing on the White House lawn.

(c) Mark Twain said that the reports of his death were "greatly exaggerated."

5. paean

(a) A sudden, stabbing pain in my side caused me to double over.

(b) The two-hundred-voice choir sang, "This Land Is Your Land."

(c) My boss thanked me for the way I had handled the McQuarry matter.

6. svelte

(a) Her witty reviews made her the most popular of New York critics.

(b) Lunch consisted of carrot sticks, spinach, whole wheat bread, a tomato, grated carrots and a helping of cottage cheese.

(c) I couldn't resist the smooth feel of the soft leather jacket.

7. acerbic

(a) The dark clouds on the horizon threatened stormy weather.

(b) "No way!" was Anita's response to my offer of help.

(c) A small amount of citric acid gives the drink its tart taste.

8. sartorial

(a) The latest issue of the magazine is devoted to men's fashions.

(b) "Thanks for your help," she said, even though I'd done nothing.

(c) The book *Dress for Success* is full of suggestions for people interested in succeeding in the corporate world.

9. repartee

(a) We roared at the dummy's responses to the ventriloquist's remarks.

(b) "Excuse me," he said as he interrupted my response.

(c) It annoys me that every time I ask a question, she replies with a question.

10. repine

(a) I said, "Don't apologize; you couldn't help it."

(b) We were uncertain about what might have put Antonia in such a melancholy mood.

(c) She was feeling tired, so she decided to lie down for an hour or so.

14E Narrative

Read the narrative below; then complete the exercise that follows it.

HEPBURN FROM A TO Z

Her first big part came in 1928 when she was twenty-one, in a pre-Broadway try-out of a play called *The Big Pond.* Confident, but naïve, she **misconstrued** the silence of the other actors after the performance as awe in the presence of greatness. Not until the next day did she learn that her acting was so lackluster that the management had fired her. The other actors had been silent out of pure embarrassment.

Such a crashing failure could have been the end of a career, but not for the stalwart Katharine Hepburn. Persistence was her forte. Sixty-six years, four Academy Awards for best actress, and more than fifty films later, Miss Hepburn was still performing. This time, the woman long known as the Queen of Hollywood was the star of *One Christmas,* a two-hour television special. At eighty-seven, she was, as always, **svelte** in the tailored slacks that were her **sartorial** trademark; and she still moved with ease and grace despite an artificial right hip. At a time when another might have been in her **dotage,** Miss Hepburn's mind and acting skills were as sharp as ever.

To Katharine Hepburn, setbacks were merely obstacles to overcome in a stage and screen career that had many ups and downs. And Hepburn bore no grudges. On one occasion, Dorothy Parker, a critic famous for her **acerbic** wit, wrote in her review of the Broadway play *The Lake*: "Katharine Hepburn runs the gamut of emotion from A to B." Later, Hepburn generously commented, "Dorothy Parker was right."

In Hollywood, Hepburn made a string of pictures while under contract to RKO studios; however, she found her roles **insipid,** a circumstance intolerable to an independent-thinking, Bryn Mawr–educated woman. A notable exception was the last of her pictures with RKO, *Bringing Up Baby,* in which she costarred with Cary Grant. The **debonair** Grant in his customary white tie and tails was a perfect foil for the strong-willed and opinionated Hepburn, and the **repartee** between the two stars struck sparks on the screen. Still, friction between Hepburn and the studio increased because RKO **foisted** upon her even more unsuitable roles. Then, in 1937, unwilling to **deign** to appear in more films that she found unacceptable, she bought out her contract for a quarter of a million dollars. The studio almost destroyed her career with the **canard** that "Hepburn was box-office poison," but the success of *The Philadelphia Story,* in which she had starred on Broadway and whose movie rights she co-owned, gave this woman of classic beauty, intelligence, and strong character the creative independence she craved.

In 1942 Hepburn made *Woman of the Year* with Spencer Tracy. It is the first of nine movies in which they appear together. Their first meeting was memorable. Hepburn, wearing high heels, was slightly taller than he was. "I'm afraid I'm a little tall for you, Mr. Tracy," Hepburn said. "Don't worry, Miss Hepburn," Tracy replied, "I'll cut you down to my size." The relationship—both professional and personal—was described by Hepburn as "absolute bliss" and lasted until Tracy's death in 1967.

Hepburn was not one to **repine**. She once said, "If you get handed a tragedy, you have to face it with character." She continued her work in films and on stage thinking of the present rather than the past. When she was interviewed after completing *One Christmas*, she was asked if she would watch it. She indicated that she would not and explained with words that summed up her entire life. "I've done it, and there's nothing I can do about it now."

In 1991, Katharine Hepburn published her autobiography, *Me*, which she wrote in longhand without benefit of a ghost writer. Part of its appeal was its immediacy; the text read as though she were addressing the reader directly in her crackling New England twang with every syllable clearly articulated. It won **paeans** from the public, who instantly made it a bestseller. If its title seemed **narcissistic**, Hepburn was unapologetic. No one had ever accused her of false modesty; conversely, she often expressed a level-headed estimation of herself, saying once that she is "revered rather like an old building." Of her own admission, this complex woman has said that it was her **overweening** ambition to be famous, to be a star, that led her to the theater in the first place.

Answer each of the following questions in a sentence. Whenever a vocabulary word does not appear in the question, try to use one (or a form of one) in your answer. In a few cases, both question and answer may contain vocabulary words.

1. How did **narcissism** lead to a misunderstanding early in Hepburn's career?

   _____

2. To what can Hepburn's continued success be attributed?

   _____

3. Where in the narrative is there evidence of Hepburn's high standards?

   _____

4. Why can Dorothy Parker's comment about Hepburn be characterized as **acerbic**?

   _____

5. In what way did RKO offend Hepburn's sense of independence?

   _____

6. What do Grant's white tie and tails and Hepburn's slacks have in common?

   _____

7. If Hepburn and Grant "struck sparks on the screen," what would be a likely response from movie critics and the public?

   _____

8. Why could Hepburn have worn the same slacks in her eighties that she wore in her forties?

   _____

9. How would you describe Hepburn and Tracy's first meeting?

   _____

10. If Hepburn had **repined** over Tracy's death, how might her career have been affected?

    _____

11. What would be an appropriate response to a report that Hepburn in her mid-eighties was in her **dotage**?

    _____

WORDLY WISE

A **canard** is a false and deliberately mis-leading story circulated to deceive others. The term probably derives from the French word *canard*, " duck." There is a saying in France, *vendre un canard a moitie*, which can be translated as "to half sell a duck," meaning not to sell it at all! This phrase is a French idiom for trickery; one craftily obtains money from the sale of the duck but still retains ownership of it.

A **narcissistic** person is one who exhibits excessive self-regard and self-love. The term goes back to the Greek myth of Narcissus, a youth who saw his reflection in a pool of water and promptly fell in love with himself. The unfortunate youth pined away and was about to die when the gods took pity on him and turned him into the flower that bears his name.

Lesson 15

Word List
Study the definitions of the words below; then do the exercises for the lesson.

anachronism
ə naˊ krə ni zəm

n. **1.** The placing of some person or thing out of its proper historical place.
[In a play set in 1922, a television onstage would be an *anachronism*.]
2. A person or thing that is or seems to be out of its proper time in history.
[The personal computer has made the typewriter an *anachronism*.]

apiary
āˊ pē er ē

n. A place where bees are raised for their honey.
[Beekeepers wear special protective clothing when visiting the *apiary*.]

archetype
ärˊ ki tīp

n. **1.** The original model from which others are made or developed.
[Ford's Model-T was the *archetype* for mass-produced automobiles.]
2. Patterns of myth and ritual that occur repeatedly in diverse cultures throughout time.
[In his much-respected book *Hero with a Thousand Faces,* Joseph Campbell traces the hero *archetype* across cultures and centuries up to the present day.]

carcinogen
kärˊ si nə jən

n. A substance that causes cancer.
[Research has clearly established the presence of *carcinogens* in tobacco products.]
carcinogenic *adj.*

checkered
chəˊ kərd

adj. Marked by frequent changes of situation; full of ups and downs.
[She has had a *checkered* business career, but her credo is "When the going gets tough, the tough get going."]

cornucopia
kôr nə kōˊ pē ə

n. **1.** A goat's horn, or a straw container shaped like it, filled with produce from the harvest; a horn of plenty.
[Thanksgiving greeting cards often show images of *cornucopias* as table centerpieces.]
2. An enormous store; an abundance.
[The Modern Library series offers a *cornucopia* of literary classics.]

devolve
di välvˊ

v. To pass on or be passed on to.
[When President John F. Kennedy was assassinated, presidential duties *devolved* upon Vice President Lyndon B. Johnson.]

equitable
eˊ kwə tə bəl

adj. Fair to all concerned.
[The teachers' contract will be not be signed until its terms seem *equitable* to all the parties.]

exigencies
ekˊ sə jən sēz

n. pl. Demands; requirements.
[The *exigencies* of a faltering economy call for action by governmental leaders.]

fatalism
fā təl isˊ tik

n. The belief that fate determines everything and one cannot influence the outcome of particular events.
["Whatever will be, will be" is an expression of *fatalism*.]
fatalistic *adj.*

gustatory gəs´ tə tōr ē	*adj.* Relating to the sense of taste. [The chocolate layer cake in the display case was both a visual and a *gustatory* delight.]
minutiae mə noō´ shē e	*n. pl.* Small details. ["He cannot see the forest for the trees" is a metaphorical expression indicating that one is so involved in *minutiae* that he fails to see the larger picture.]
motley mät´ lē	*adj.* Composed of many different kinds or types; diverse. [The band members were a *motley* group who expressed their sartorial taste in a variety of unconventional ways.]
prospectus prə spek´ təs	*n.* A printed statement, given to potential buyers, describing a business or investment opportunity. [The *prospectus* of the mutual fund apprises investors of the stocks it selects.]
vernal vʉr´ nəl	*adj.* Of or relating to the spring. [The *vernal* equinox occurs on or about March 21 and marks the beginning of spring in the northern hemisphere.]

15A Understanding Meanings

Read the sentences in each group below. If a sentence correctly uses the word in boldface, write C on the line of the corresponding number below the group. If a sentence is incorrect, rewrite it so that the vocabulary word in boldface is used correctly.

■ 1. A **cornucopia** is a horn filled to overflowing with fruit, grain, and flowers.
2. An **apiary** is a place where birds are housed.
3. A **checkered** life is one marked by great shifts in fortune.
4. A **prospectus** is a view over a wide area.
5. A **vernal** pool is one that is fed by an underground spring.

1. _____
2. _____
3. _____
4. _____
5. _____

■ 6. **Minutiae** are very brief intervals of time.
7. An **anachronism** is something out of its proper chronological order.
8. A **motley** collection is one that is untidy and disheveled.
9. To **devolve** authority is to delegate it to another.
10. **Exigencies** are emergency exits.

6. _____

7. _____

8. _____

9. _____

10. _____

■ 11. An **archetype** is a perfect example of a particular type.
12. A **gustatory** treat is one that comes as a surprise.
13. **Carcinogenic** compounds are substances that cause cancer.
14. **Fatalism** is a death caused by an accident or disaster.
15. An **equitable** arrangement is one that is fair to all concerned.

11. _____

12. _____

13. _____

14. _____

15. _____

15B Using Words

If the word (or a form of the word) in boldface fits in a sentence in the group below it, write the word in the blank space. If the word does not fit, leave the space empty.

1. **archetype**
   (a) Penicillin was the _____ for antibiotics used to fight infection.
   (b) Antigone, of Sophocles' tragic drama, is the _____ of the Greek heroine.
   (c) If you're in the market for a new car, the Z-Turbo is the very latest _____ .

2. **exigencies**
   (a) The _____ of Arctic travel make keeping warm the first priority.
   (b) I regret that the _____ of party strife keep good people out of politics.
   (c) The _____ of fame require one to keep a level head.

3. **anachronism**
   (a) It is an _____ to say that 1900 was a leap year.
   (b) Desdemona's wristwatch was a glaring _____ in the production of *Othello*.
   (c) By the mid 1800s, the railroads had made the stagecoach an _____ .

4. **fatalistic**
   (a) The thieves made a _____ mistake by returning to the scene of the crime.
   (b) Diseases that were once _____ can now be cured quickly.
   (c) "It has to turn out poorly" expresses a _____ attitude.

5. **checkered**
   (a) After his last long-distance meet, he said he was too _____ to celebrate his victory.
   (b) I lost the game when she _____ me.
   (c) After a _____ first season, Theater One began building a loyal audience.

6. **motley**
   (a) A _____ assortment of townspeople and students gathered in the park on Earth Day.
   (b) Her "poem" seemed a _____ collection of unconnected words and phrases.
   (c) The stock-car racer at the Indianapolis 500 hoped to see the _____ pattern of the winner's flag.

7. **prospectus**
   (a) The _____ from the front of the house includes a fine view of the river.
   (b) I need time to peruse the _____ before deciding whether or not to invest.
   (c) The _____ of doubling our money in a year is slim.

8. **devolve**
   (a) If I have to leave, responsibility for the project's success will _____ upon you.
   (b) The plot seems to _____ around identical twins and their telepathic powers.
   (c) Since the committee ceased to have a function, the mayor decided to _____ it.

15C Synonyms, Antonyms, Analogies

Each group of four words below contains two words that are either synonyms or antonyms. Circle these two words; then circle the S if they are synonyms, the A if they are antonyms.

1. ANACHRONISM   ORIGINAL
   HABITUE   ARCHETYPE   S   A

2. FRACTIOUS   MOTLEY
   HOMOGENEOUS   VERNAL   S   A

3. CALUMNIES   DEMANDS
   EXIGENCIES   MINUTIAE   S   A

4. UNEVENTFUL   CHECKERED
   GUSTATORY   FRIGHTFUL   S   A

5. DETAILS   CARCINOGENS
   MINUTIAE   PORTALS   S   A

Complete the analogies by selecting the pair of words whose relationship most resembles the relationship of the pair in capital letters. Circle the letter in front of the pair you choose.

6. APIARY : HONEY ::
   (a) orchard : fruit
   (b) milk : cream
   (c) chicken : eggs
   (d) stable : horses

7. VERNAL : SPRING ::
   (a) annual : season
   (b) casual : summer
   (c) autumnal : fall
   (d) frigid : winter

8. GUSTATORY : TASTE ::
   (a) fragrant : smell
   (b) bourgeois : class
   (c) palpable : touch
   (d) cacophonous : hearing

9. FATALISTIC : HOROSCOPE ::
   (a) affluent : wealth
   (b) salubrious : health
   (c) patriotic : flag
   (d) auspicious : seer

10. EQUITABLE : DISCRIMINATORY ::
    (a) motley : checkered
    (b) inhibited : overweening
    (c) veritable : antagonistic
    (d) aggrieved : stultifying

15D Images of Words

Circle the letter of each sentence that suggests the numbered boldface vocabulary word. In each group, you may circle more than one letter or none at all.

1. **cornucopia**
(a) Carved above the doorway was a ram's horn overflowing with fruit.
(b) American factories rushed to satisfy the huge demand for consumer goods.
(c) The fertile farmlands of the valley provide a rich harvest of vegetables.

2. gustatory

(a) The sensitive tips of the fingers are used to read Braille.

(b) Nerves from the tongue convey the sensation of taste to the brain.

(c) The wind picked up by evening, reaching gusts of 40–45 mph.

3. apiary

(a) The cages that confine them are large enough to permit the birds to fly.

(b) The Cleghorns sell the excess honey they get from their hives.

(c) The gorilla is the largest of the great apes.

4. minutiae

(a) Cheese mites are too small to be seen with the naked eye.

(b) No aspect of her business was too small for Ms. Liu's attention.

(c) I took care of the numerous details involved in running the travel agency.

5. equitable

(a) Women doing the same work as men should receive the same pay.

(b) Two times twelve is equal to four times six.

(c) The rules for admission to the college are the same for all applicants.

6. fatalism

(a) Scientists are debating whether the crew of the sunken submarine can survive.

(b) We don't worry; we will accept whatever fate has in store for us.

(c) The emergency medical team rushed her to the hospital, thinking she was a victim of fatalism.

7. devolve

(a) After the vice president, next in line for the presidency is the Speaker of the House.

(b) Charles is the oldest, followed by me, and then my younger sister Joan.

(c) According to this theory, plants and animals have their origins in preexisting types.

8. vernal

(a) My favorite time of year is when the crocuses and daffodils begin to appear.

(b) The hours of daylight equaled and then exceeded the length of the nights.

(c) The first snowstorms usually arrived by November or early December.

9. carcinogen

(a) Large doses of saccharine produced malignant tumors in laboratory mice.

(b) Malaria is caused by the bite of an infected female anopheles mosquito.

(c) Asbestos has been identified as a cancer-causing agent.

10. anachronism

(a) The car is five years old, so it's time to trade it in for a new one.

(b) Pushbutton telephones have largely replaced the rotary kind.

(c) Old Mr. Percy seems out of touch with the modern world.

15E Narrative

Read the narrative below; then complete the exercise that follows it.

FARMING FOR GOOD FOOD AND FELLOWSHIP

The sturdily independent farmer, working the family farm passed from generation to generation, is a familiar American **archetype**. In 1900, when it took 30 million people to feed a population of 75 million, four out of every ten Americans lived on farms. The United States Department of Agriculture stopped counting farm families in 1993. However, by 2000, reliable estimates indicate that the number of farm families had fallen to fewer than one in fifty; about four-and-one-half million people were feeding a United States population of well over 250 million. The **exigencies** of a changing nation—one that faces a restructured economy and prefers an easier physical life, higher income, and urban advantages—favor fewer but larger and more mechanized farms. Many small farmers took a **fatalistic** view, believing that the small family farm had become an **anachronism**.

Robyn Van En thought otherwise. In the mid 1980s, she was managing the small Indian Line Farm in South Egremont, Massachusetts. At that time, a friend from Switzerland told her about *Teikei,* a name suggesting "food with the farmer's face on it." This concept was developed in the 1960s by a group of Japanese women dissatisfied with the increasing importation of food and the decreasing number of farms and farmers in their communities. Realizing that the Japanese and Swiss models aligned with her philosophy, Robyn decided to apply them to her own operation, naming it Community Sponsored Agriculture. She began by publishing a **prospectus,** inviting consumers to pay part of her farm costs in return for a proportionate share of its produce. The enthusiastic response she received led to the formation of the first CSA group in the United States. Robyn became a pioneer by proclaiming the "fruits" of such farming, and the movement spread.

By 1995, there were about four hundred groups nationwide, ranging in size from four to as many as one thousand members. Typically, a CSA core group draws up a budget reflecting all costs for the year. The projected annual expenses and the number of members in the project determine the price of each share. Through their shares, members receive fresh food; through their participation, they experience community, and through negotiation, farms take advantage of the biodiversity of their areas. For example, one group might wish to start an **apiary**, while another might want to look into keeping a small flock of sheep for their wool and meat.

Sometimes members with busy lives fail to fulfill their quotas and the work **devolves** onto other participants. This can lead to ill will and instability. Although some groups have disbanded, creating a **checkered** past for the CSA, on the whole, the CSA movement has shown a healthy growth. As of 2000, there were more than one thousand CSA groups across the United States and Canada.

Jill Agnew, of Willow Pond Farm in Sabattus, Maine, runs a typical CSA operation with seventy members. They come from all social classes and are of all ages; their only common bond is a love of fresh produce. On "picking days," this **motley** group gathers on Agnew's farm to get their share of whichever of the thirty-five kinds of vegetables are at their peak that day. Flowers are also there for the picking, and an **equitable** system of distribution ensures that each gets a fair share, depending on the amount of work done and the varied preferences for different kinds of produce.

Many CSA groups offer their members the opportunity to pay their whole share or part of their share by working on the premises, and some require it. The Rose Valley Farm outside Rochester, New York, expects its one hundred members to contribute two hours of work a week, in addition to weekly dues of seven to fourteen dollars. This work ranges from the **minutiae** of some office duties to working in the fields.

CSA groups flourish when everyone benefits. Farmers get a guaranteed income to pay for seeds, equipment, and labor, and they greatly reduce the waste that results from unsold produce. The members get freshly picked vegetables that offer a **gustatory** treat unknown to those who depend on supermarket produce, picked days before and trucked across the country. Since CSA farms do not use chemicals, which may be **carcinogenic**, members have the further advantage of knowing that they and their families are eating only organically grown vegetables.

From the time when the early lettuces and radishes come to perfection in the warmth of the **vernal** sun until October brings its **cornucopia** of pumpkins and winter squash, members get a deep satisfaction from having an intimate involvement with the land. They know that in helping themselves, they are also helping to preserve the tradition of the small, family-owned farm. That perhaps is the greatest satisfaction of all.

Answer each of the following questions in a sentence. Whenever a vocabulary word does not appear in the question, try to use one (or a form of one) in your answer. In a few cases, both the question and the answer may contain vocabulary words.

1. What would be the essential elements of a Community Sponsored Agriculture **prospectus**?

   _____

2. What promise does the **cornucopia** of fresh farm vegetables offer?

   _____

3. Why does the small farm have such a powerful hold on the imagination?

_____

4. Why would the **vernal** sunshine be especially welcome to CSA members in colder climates?

_____

5. What health benefit can CSA members claim?

_____

6. What would have happened if all farmers had assumed a **fatalistic** attitude when modern life began affecting agricultural methods?

_____

7. Why are CSA members sometimes expected to perform a set number of hours of work?

_____

8. What would you expect to be a primary concern of CSA members?

_____

9. Give examples of two kinds of office work likely to be performed at a CSA Operation.

_____

10. How is it suggested that the CSA movement has not enjoyed unqualified success?

_____

11. Why would it be impossible to describe a typical CSA member?

_____

12. What might CSA members with a taste for honey do?

_____

WORDLY WISE

The Greek prefix *ana-*, "backward," and the Greek root *kronos*, "time," combine to form **anachronism**, "something that exists outside of its proper time frame." Several other words share this root. A *chronometer* is an accurate instrument for measuring time. A *chronic* illness is one that lasts a long time. *Synchronous* events occur at precisely the same time. A *chronicle* is a detailed account of events over time. Items listed in *chronological* order are listed according to the time at which they occurred.

According to Greek mythology, Zeus, king of the gods, was nursed as a baby by a she-goat, and his special relationship with this animal has given rise to two English words.

The first is *aegis,* which originally meant "shield" and now means any form of protection. Zeus's shield was of goatskin (*aigis* in Greek). The second word is **cornucopia,** which means "horn of plenty." According to the Greek myth, one of the goat's horns broke off and miraculously filled with fruit to provide sustenance for Zeus.

Court jesters in medieval times wore suits of contrasting patches of color; such attire was called **motley** (in Middle English, *motlei* means variegated cloth). Their incongruous appearance was intended to provoke laughter. The term has survived as an adjective and retains its essential meaning, "having elements of great variety or incongruity."

Lesson 16

Word List

Study the definitions of the words below; then do the exercises for the lesson.

apocalyptic
ə pä kə lip´ tik

adj. Involving or predicting disastrous, uncontrollable events.
[Cyberpunk literature, a form of science fiction, suggests an *apocalyptic* future of an impersonal world saturated with complex technology.]

concatenation
kän ka tə nā´ shən

n. A joining or linking together of elements.
[A *concatenation* of serendipitous happenings resulted in my best vacation ever.]

convulse
kən vəls´

v. To shake or cause to shake suddenly and violently.
[Audiences *convulsed* with laughter at the entertainer's unique mixture of comedy and magic.]
convulsion   *n.*   1. An abnormal, strong, and uncontrollable muscle seizure.
[The *convulsions* she once experienced because of epilepsy are now controlled by medication.]
2. A violent disturbance.
[The *convulsions* that the stock market had experienced for three days were brought under control by closing it early.]

decree
di krē´

n. An order or decision which, according to its author, must be obeyed.
[The city council's *decree* imposing a 10 P.M. curfew is being challenged in court.]
decree   *v.*

expatriate
ek spā´ trē āt (v)
ek spā´ trē ət (n)

n. One who leaves his or her country to live elsewhere.
[Seattle's Saigon restaurants are popular with Vietnamese *expatriates*.]
expatriate   *v.*

fetid
fe´ təd

adj. Smelling very bad; stinking.
[We discovered that the *fetid* smell was coming from eggs we had forgotten to refrigerate.]

holocaust
hō´ lə kôst

n.   1. A catastrophic event resulting in widespread loss of life.
[Many people feared that the world was on the brink of a nuclear *holocaust* during the 1962 Cuban missile crisis.]
2. Widespread destruction caused by fire.
[Each day, we were dismayed at the news of the *holocaust* in the forest fires of the West.]

infraction
in frak´ shən

n. A violation or breaking of a rule.
[Police officers normally issue a warning for minor traffic *infractions*.]

insouciance
in soo´ sē əns

n. Freedom from concern; lighthearted lack of awareness.
[His *insouciance* toward criticism was due to his overweening narcissism.]
insouciant   *adj.*

minion
min´ yən

n. A slavish follower, attendant, or supporter.
[None of the mayor's *minions* were willing to tell him of the secret investigation into his campaign finances.]

sanguinary	*adj.* **1.** Involving much bloodshed or killing.
saṅ´ gwe ner ē	[Gettysburg was the most *sanguinary* of all the Civil War battles.]
	2. Bloodthirsty; cruel.
	[When India was partitioned at independence, both Hindus and Muslims carried out *sanguinary* attacks on the other.]
staccato	*adj.* Broken up into short, sharp bursts.
stə kä´ tō	[The *staccato* tapping of the woodpecker awakened me this morning.]
sybaritic	*adj.* Marked by extravagant pleasure and luxury.
si bə ri´ tik	[Photographs of the *sybaritic* lifestyles of the rich and famous are hallmarks of this glossy magazine.]
thespian	*n.* An actor or actress.
thəs´ pē ən	[Her compelling desire to become an accomplished *thespian* led her apply to the prestigious drama school.]
verisimilitude	*n.* The quality of appearing true; depicting realism.
ver ə sə mi´ lə tōōd	[The book's *verisimilitude* cannot be questioned by anyone familiar with the events it describes.]

16A Understanding Meanings

Read the sentences in each group below. If a sentence correctly uses the word in boldface, write C on the line of the corresponding number below the group. If a sentence is incorrect, rewrite it so that the vocabulary word in boldface is used correctly.

■ 1. A **sybaritic** lifestyle is one marked by excessive indulgence of the senses.
2. **Verisimilitude** is the quality of being comparable.
3. An **insouciant** person is one who is blithely unconcerned.
4. A **convulsion** is a sudden and violent motion.
5. A **thespian** is a person who travels about doing odd jobs.

1. _____
2. _____
3. _____
4. _____
5. _____

■ 6. A **holocaust** is an event marked by great destruction.
7. A **fetid** room is one that hasn't been refurnished for many years.
8. A **sanguinary** ruler is one who sheds blood.
9. A **minion** is a small quantity or amount.
10. To **expatriate** people is to send them out of the country.

6. _____

7. _____

8. _____

9. _____

10. _____

■ 11. An **apocalyptic** story is one that has dubious authenticity.
12. A **decree** is a step in a graduated series.
13. An **infraction** is the breaching of a law, rule, or agreement.
14. A **concatenation** is a series of linked events.
15. A **staccato** delivery is one that is brief and to the point.

11. _____

12. _____

13. _____

14. _____

15. _____

16B Using Words

If the word (or a form of the word) in boldface fits in a sentence in the group below it, write the word in the blank space. If the word does not fit, leave the space empty.

1. **convulsions**
   (a) We filmed the earth's _____ during the great Mexican earthquake.
   (b) The story about their trip had so many _____ that we were sure they were exaggerating.
   (c) The king's abdication caused political _____ in the nation's capital.

2. **staccato**
   (a) The opera begins with a _____ drumbeat followed by a loud trumpet blast.
   (b) The _____ sounds of heavy rain on the metal roof kept me awake.
   (c) I could tell she was nervous because she spoke in short _____ bursts.

3. **decree**
   (a) It is the sheriff's responsibility to enforce the court's _____ .
   (b) In the absence of a representative democracy, the czar ruled by _____ .
   (c) The young child said she wanted to go to college to get a _____ in math.

4. **sanguinary**
   (a) Meredith's _____ temperament made her a popular person to work with.
   (b) The _____ conflict in Rwanda resulted in the displacement or death of a majority of the population.
   (c) The setting sun tinged the western sky a _____ hue.

5. **verisimilitude**
   (a) Georgina bears a striking _____ to her cousin Rosa.
   (b) There is not a scrap of _____ to anything she said.
   (c) The painting's _____ to nature is its most striking feature.

6. **apocalyptic**
   (a) The movie's _____ final scene portrays the destruction of the world.
   (b) The rumor that our science teacher Ms. Gregerson had won the lottery was _____ .
   (c) Some people feared that _____ events would occur at the end of the millennium.

7. **fetid**
   (a) _____ piles of garbage were piled up in the streets, awaiting collection.
   (b) Horace's group of friends _____ him for his birthday.
   (c) We _____ the dog in the yard when the guests began to arrive.

8. **minions**
   (a) Terri's racing time met the _____ requirement for competing in the marathon.
   (b) _____ of bison grazed on the prairie as far as the eye could see.
   (c) In order to enter the queen's presence, one had first to get past her _____ .

16C Synonyms, Antonyms, Analogies

Each group of four words below contains two words that are either synonyms or antonyms. Circle these two words; then circle the S if they are synonyms, the A if they are antonyms.

1. FETID   INSIPID
   BENEVOLENT   SANGUINARY   S   A

2. MINION   DILETTANTE
   CONCATENATION FOLLOWER   S   A

3. STACCATO   SYBARITIC

    UNRULY   ASCETIC   S   A

4. VERISIMILITUDE   CONCATENATION

    FALSITY   PROSPECTUS   S   A

5. DECREE   CANARD

    SPASM   CONVULSION   S   A

Complete the analogies by selecting the pair of words whose relationship most resembles the relationship of the pair in capital letters. Circle the letter in front of the pair you choose.

6. DIRE : APOCALYPTIC ::
   - (a) amorphous : svelte
   - (b) risible : solemn
   - (c) bad : rotten
   - (d) frugal : prodigal

7. THESPIAN : STAGE ::
   - (a) musician : instrument
   - (b) protagonist : novel
   - (c) aborigine : domain
   - (d) orator : podium

8. FETID : SMELL ::
   - (a) brackish : taste
   - (b) harmonious : sound
   - (c) vacuous : talk
   - (d) palpable : touch

9. EXPATRIATE : LEAVES ::
   - (a) pioneer : initiates
   - (b) author : publishes
   - (c) exponent : instructs
   - (d) immigrant : migrates

10. IMPROPRIETY : INFRACTION ::
   - (a) archetype : model
   - (b) mandate : decree
   - (c) misbehavior : disobedience
   - (d) depredation : tribulation

16D Images of Words

Circle the letter of each sentence that suggests the numbered boldface vocabulary word. In each group, you may circle more than one letter or none at all.

1. **expatriate**
   - (a) Barnaby loves to talk at length about how successful his children are.
   - (b) After fifty years in America, Yolande still had plans to return to Mexico.
   - (c) Americans living in Paris during the 1920s formed a close-knit community.

2. apocalyptic
(a) Mr. Brown was enraged when he saw the gate had been left open.
(b) The singers' voices blended together in sweet harmony.
(c) The diver's condition was so serious he was rushed to the emergency room.

3. verisimilitude
(a) The novel very accurately describes the streets of Dublin.
(b) I believe her when she says she never tells a lie.
(c) The Simoglous were looking for a painting that would match the colors of their new sofa.

4. convulse
(a) The professor shook her student's hand enthusiastically as he accepted the award.
(b) The patient's heart gave an erratic reading on the electrocardiogram.
(c) A smile brightened Eliza's face when she learned that she would perform a solo in the concert.

5. sybaritic
(a) Grace's legs were so weak that she could walk only with difficulty.
(b) On our vacation, we went to the ocean every day.
(c) Each guest at the spa was attended by a personal trainer.

6. insouciance
(a) They walked past the doorman as though they were guests at the exclusive hotel.
(b) Groucho Marx's innocent manner enabled him get away with the most outrageous things.
(c) The souffle was so light that it melted in my mouth.

7. holocaust
(a) When they took the turkey from the oven, they saw it had been burned to a crisp.
(b) The Great Fire of London in 1666 virtually destroyed the city.
(c) Nazi book burnings consigned thousands of great works to the flames.

8. thespian
(a) I tried to act happy when I learned that our vacation would be spent camping.
(b) She learned to act at the Royal Academy of Dramatic Art.
(c) Ronald Reagan was a screen actor before entering politics.

9. concatenation
(a) The yowling of cats outside my window made sleep almost impossible.
(b) One thing led to another, and before I knew it I was in charge of planning the dance.
(c) Strings of lights in the trees made the park into a fairyland at night.

10. infraction
(a) When the pebble struck the car, it caused a slight crack in the windshield.
(b) Had I been aware that talking was forbidden, I would have kept quiet.
(c) Four-fifths is 0.8 when expressed as a decimal.

16E Narrative

Read the narrative below; then complete the exercise that follows it.

A CAMBODIAN ODYSSEY

Haing Ngor did not think of himself as a **thespian**; he was a medical doctor hardly accustomed to the **sybaritic** trappings of the rich and well known. Yet, there he was at the fifty-seventh annual Academy Awards holding an Oscar for best supporting actor in *The Killing Fields,* a film showing the **apocalyptic** events of the late 1970s in his native Cambodia. The **concatenation** of circumstances that had brought him to the stage of the Dorothy Chandler Pavilion would itself have made a film to strain any moviegoer's credulity. It's not surprising, therefore, that when asked by a reporter afterward how he felt, Dr. Ngor was unable to answer immediately.

Ten years before, in 1975, he had been a successful physician in Phnom Penh, the capital of Cambodia. Although not **insouciant**, Dr. Ngor, because of his family's wealth and his own ample income, was removed from the civil war that had raged in the countryside for the past five years between the guerilla leader Pol Pot's communist Khmer Rouge rebels and the government forces.

Then, his shelter was shattered on April 17, 1975, when Dr. Ngor heard the **staccato** sounds of gunfire coming from within his hospital. Suddenly, Khmer Rouge rebels burst into the operating theater, and one fighter, no more than twelve years old, pointed a gun at his head and demanded, "You doctor?" Pol Pot had **decreed** that every educated Cambodian must die in order to bring a new Cambodia into existence. Dr. Ngor shook his head and said that the doctor had fled. By doing so he saved his life, but the unconscious patient was left to die.

What followed defies belief. Pol Pot's **minions**, often children barely in their teens armed with automatic weapons, went on a killing spree. The people of Phnom Penh were driven from their homes and into the countryside to work as slave laborers. Private property was abolished and all ownership records were destroyed. People were killed for the slightest **infraction** of Communist party rules. Dr. Ngor was captured and later sentenced to death for addressing his fiancée Chang My Huoy as "sweetheart" instead of "comrade lady" and again for "counter-revolutionary activity" (eating leaves he had picked). He survived because his captors simply forgot about him or were too lazy to carry out the sentences. He spent months in a **fetid** prison where he was repeatedly tortured but was one day released with no explanation. His parents and other family members disappeared without a trace, and Chang My Huoy died of starvation in his arms on June 2, 1978.

Pol Pot's **sanguinary** rule ended in 1979 when Vietnamese forces invaded Cambodia, defeated the Khmer Rouge, and drove its leader into exile. Mass executions and famine had killed three million Cambodians. Of the country's five hundred doctors, fewer than fifty survived, among them Dr. Ngor. In the confusion that followed the Vietnamese invasion, he escaped to Thailand and from there made his way to the United States.

Unable to practice medicine, he did relief work among the Cambodian **expatriate** community in Los Angeles. It was there that he was spotted by a casting director for a movie being made about the Cambodian **holocaust.** He played Dith Pran, a Cambodian interpreter for *New York Times* correspondent Sydney Schanberg, author of the book about Cambodia on which the movie was based. The **verisimilitude** of the film was affirmed by Dr. Ngor and Dith Pran, whose experiences in Cambodia had been remarkably similar. It had an extraordinary effect on those who saw it, opening their eyes for the first time to the horrors of Pol Pot's regime.

Winning the Oscar had given Dr. Ngor a unique opportunity to tell the world of the agony that had **convulsed** his country, and he later wrote a book about his experiences. But when he looked at the reporter who asked the question after the Academy Awards presentation, all he could say in reply was, "You ask me, 'Doctor, how do you feel?' Such pain I have you cannot imagine."

Then in 1996, in a terrible final irony, Haing Ngor, a survivor of the killing fields of Cambodia, became the murder victim of a gang, thought by many to be high on crack cocaine, outside his Los Angeles apartment. Robbery was the motive, and the three men were later convicted and received long prison sentences. By a curious coincidence, the day that the three separate juries returned their verdicts was also the day that Cambodia announced the death of Pol Pot.

Answer each of the following questions in a sentence. Whenever a vocabulary word does not appear in the question, try to use one (or a form of one) in your answer. In a few cases, both question and answer may contain vocabulary words.

1. How would you describe the values of most of the people gathered at the Dorothy Chandler Pavilion?

2. Did Dr. Ngor's privileged position allow him to block out the pain of his fellow Cambodians? Explain your answer.

3. What began the **concatenation** that cost Dr. Ngor his privileged status?

4. What did Hitler and Pol Pot have in common?

5. How did Pol Pot govern when he controlled Cambodia?

    _____

6. What do World War Two and Pol Pot's rule over Cambodia have in common?

    _____

7. How did Dr. Ngor recognize the sound of machine-gun fire?

    _____

8. Under Pol Pot, what kinds of offenses brought the death penalty?

    _____

9. What would be the effect of overcrowding and unsanitary conditions in the prisons?

    _____

10. What helped Dr. Ngor feel at home in Los Angeles?

    _____

11. How did Dr. Ngor become a **thespian?**

    _____

12. What encomium did Dr. Ngor and Dith Pran give the movie?

    _____

WORDLY WISE

The original meaning of **holocaust**, from the Greek *holokausten*, "completely burned," comes from biblical references to the religious sacrifice of animals burned on an altar. In the seventeenth century, the meaning broadened to "wholesale destruction by fire." In the twentieth century, **Holocaust** came to mean "the wholesale destruction of a people," referring to the murder of millions of Jews and others by the Nazis during World War II. In this meaning, the word is capitalized to emphasize the significance of that crime against humanity.

Sybaris, one of the first Greek colonies, was established in southern Italy around 800 B.C. The soil was fertile, and the people of Sybaris became wealthy and enjoyed lives of ease and indolence. According to legend, the Sybarites indulged in pleasure to such a degree that when the city was attacked by neighboring Crotona in 510 B.C., they were unable to defend themselves. They perished, and their city was destroyed. The Greeks preserved the term **sybarite**, perhaps as a warning, and it has passed unchanged into English.

Drama as we know it began in ancient Athens when a person stood apart from the chorus and engaged in dialogue with it. This was the first actor, reputed to have been Thespis, a Greek dramatist who lived in the sixth century B.C. His contribution to theater is acknowledged in our word **thespian**, "an actor."

Hidden Message

Write out, in the spaces provided to the right of each sentence, the words from lessons 13 through 16 that are missing in each of the sentences below. Be sure that the words you choose fit the meaning of each sentence and have the same number of letters as there are spaces. The number following each sentence gives the word list from which the missing word must be taken. If the exercise is done properly, the shaded boxes will spell out the answer to this question: "Why is experience such a hard teacher?"

1. The list at the doctor's office names each _____ in cigarette smoke. (15)

2. The man was in his _____ and made no sense. (14)

3. Profuse apologies failed to _____ my boss. (13)
4. The _____ of the situation demand action. (15)
5. Her _____ past led many to distrust her. (15)

6. The _____ performance received tepid applause. (14)
7. Don't get bogged down in the _____ of the job. (15)
8. Her _____ showed she could keep a cool head. (16)
9. That _____ about his past has been discredited. (14)
10. He's the finest _____ ever to grace the stage. (16)
11. His _____ blinds him to his many faults. (14)

12. I _____ a negative tone in his remarks. (13)

13. The _____ of the wise old man is a familiar one. (15)
14. The _____ between the two was vastly amusing. (14)
15. His _____ manner was out of place at a funeral. (13)

16. Do not _____ for your lost love. (14)

17. An entire city block was consumed in the _____ . (16)

18. Macbeth's wristwatch was an obvious _____ . (15)
19. She produced a(n) _____ of good things to eat. (15)
20. The duties _____ upon the person in charge. (15)
21. _____ ambition led to the hero's downfall. (14)

22. The three houses _____ the town square. (13)
23. I _____ you to act responsibly in this matter. (13)
24. A _____ lacks the knowledge to be called an expert. (13)

25. The _____ ship's crew needed new uniforms. (15)
26. Yielding easily to pressure is his only _____ . (13)
27. Don't _____ that old story from his past. (13)

28. You _____ the flag by trampling on it. (13)

29. We were punished for the _____ . (16)

30. I'm afraid you _____ the poem's message. (14)

31. His jokes caused us to _____ with laughter. (16)
32. Do not _____ to respond to these false charges. (14)
33. The poem is a(n) _____ to the goddess Minerva. (14)
34. We entered the town through the north _____ . (13)
35. _____ showers bring forth April's daffodils. (15)

36. Each _____ produces twenty pounds of honey. (15)

37. His _____ warnings scared the audience. (16)
38. With top hat and tails he cut a _____ figure. (14)
39. The arrangement seems _____ to all parties. (15)

40. The _____ squalor of the prison is a disgrace. (16)
41. We will _____ all those who wish to go home. (16)
42. Our tailors are devoted to _____ excellence. (14)
43. I ordered the _____ to take me to his leader. (16)

44. It is unfair to _____ schoolwork on students during vacation. (14)
45. He spoke rapidly in short _____ bursts. (16)
46. We need to _____ racism in all its forms. (13)
47. After losing twenty pounds, I feel quite _____ . (14)
48. His _____ reply showed he was still angry with us. (14)
49. Such meetings were banned by government _____ . (16)

Lesson 17

Word List

Study the definitions of the words below; then do the exercises for the lesson.

abnegate
ab ni gāt´

v. **1.** To give up as a right or claim.
[In 1947 Britain was obliged to *abnegate* its mandate to govern Palestine.]
2. To deny or renounce.
[When she *abnegated* her former position on the issue, some described her as a traitor to her party.]

ancillary
an´ sə ler ē

adj. Subordinate; less important.
[Degas was primarily a painter, and sculpture was never more than an *ancillary* activity for him.]

badinage
ba dən äzh´

n. Light, playful conversation; banter.
[When the *badinage* between the two news anchors grew tiresome, I changed the channel.]

bedizen
bi dī´ zən

v. To dress or decorate in a showy or gaudy fashion.
[The little girls, *bedizened* with beads and feathered hats, tottered about the room in their mother's high heels.]

celerity
sə ler´ ə tē

n. Speed or promptness in acting or responding.
[When the doorbell rang, he leaped off the sofa with unaccustomed *celerity*.]

cynosure
sī´ nə shôr

n. The center of attention.
[At the golf tournament, Tiger Woods was the *cynosure* of reporters and fans alike.]

itinerary
ī ti´ nə rer ē

n. **1.** The course or the planned route of a journey.
[My *itinerary* was to travel by bus from Boston to New York to Washington, D.C.]
2. A travel diary.
[Rereading my *itinerary*, I was filled with nostalgia for the great open spaces of the Midwest.]
3. A traveler's guide.
[Our Mexican *itinerary* suggested Guanajuata as a place seldom visited by tourists.]

lissome
li´ səm

adj. Moving or bending easily; supple.
[My goal is to exercise enough to become as *lissome* as my aerobics instructor.]

milieu
mēl yoo´

n. A particular social or cultural environment in which events occur.
[The author shows a remarkable familiarity with the *milieu* of Louis XIV's court.]

obstreperous
əb stre´ pə rəs

adj. Aggressively noisy or rude.
[When the guest on the television talk show became *obstreperous*, she was quickly whisked off.]

paragon
par´ ə gän

n. A model of perfection.
[The menu each day of that weekend was a *paragon* for those interested in a macrobiotic diet.]

perquisite pər´ kwə zət	*n.* An extra benefit in addition to one's regular earnings. [Free travel is a *perquisite* of being a travel agent.]
staid stād	*adj.* Lacking flamboyance; sedate; restrained. [The *staid* tunes of the 1940s suddenly seemed antediluvian when rock music burst onto the scene.]
symbiotic sim bē ä´ tik	*adj.* Mutually cooperative and beneficial. [Given the *symbiotic* relationship between fashion reporters and designers, one does not expect to find trenchant criticism of the industry in fashion magazines.] **symbiosis** *n.* Two unlike organisms living together in a close and mutually beneficial way.
tyro tī´ ro	*n.* A beginner in any field. [A former classmate of the Olympic medalist recalls her as a young *tyro* practicing in the city pool.]

17A Understanding Meanings

Read the sentences in each group below. If a sentence correctly uses the word in boldface, write C on the line of the corresponding number below the group. If a sentence is incorrect, rewrite it so that the vocabulary word in boldface is used correctly.

■ 1. An **ancillary** subject is related to but less important than the primary one.
2. A **cynosure** is something that is ominous.
3. A **paragon** is a short-tempered person.
4. To **bedizen** something is to adorn it ostentatiously.
5. An **itinerary** is the proposed route of a trip.

1. _____

2. _____

3. _____

4. _____

5. _____

■ 6. **Symbiosis** is the use of symbols to represent things.
7. A **lissome** body flexes easily.
8. A **tyro** is a tiresome person.
9. To **abnegate** something is to claim it as a right.
10. A **perquisite** is something required as a necessary condition.

6. _____

7. _____

8. _____

9. _____

10. _____

■ 11. A **milieu** is a specific setting or background.
  12. To act with **celerity** is to do so resentfully or under protest.
  13. An **obstreperous** person is one who is rude and argumentative.
  14. A **staid** person is one who eschews wild behavior.
  15. **Badinage** is the hiding of one's true purpose with intent to deceive.

11. _____

12. _____

13. _____

14. _____

15. _____

17B Using Words

If the word (or a form of the word) in boldface fits in a sentence in the group below it, write the word in the blank space. If the word does not fit, leave the space empty.

1. **bedizened**
   (a) The desperate people were _____ by false promises.
   (b) The high priests were _____ with gold ornaments sacred to the god Ra.
   (c) Pucci's models at the show were _____ with the most outrageous accessories.

2. **milieu**
   (a) The change of _____ from city tenement to Vermont farm was dramatic.
   (b) The farm workers received food and shelter in _____ of wages.
   (c) The _____ of Mexican village life is familiar to me after a year in El Rosario.

3. **symbiotic**
   (a) The program explores the _____ relationship between bees and flowers.
   (b) A complex _____ network of public and private investments holds the city together and makes it work.
   (c) The gorilla used _____ language rather than words to "talk" to humans.

4. **perquisite**
   (a) A bachelor's degree is a _____ for graduate studies at most colleges.
   (b) The relatively flimsy plane of the Wright Brothers was a _____ for all later aircraft.
   (c) The position of sales manager carries with it the _____ of a company car.

5. **lissome**
   (a) The dancers moved with the _____ grace of elegant cats.
   (b) The exercise video promises a _____ body in just thirty days.
   (c) She gave a _____ smile as she recalled the time they first met.

6. **abnegated**
   (a) The young man _____ all claims to the family fortune when he became a Buddhist monk.
   (b) Although we were losing by a score of 9 to 0, we never _____ .
   (c) As part of the Peace Plan, the invading country _____ all rights to the conquered territory.

7. **celerity**
   (a) The fire department responded with _____ to the emergency call.
   (b) There was a tone of _____ in Sylvia's voice as she announced her accomplishment.
   (c) The _____ of Pedro's fastball made him the most feared pitcher in baseball.

8. **cynosure**
   (a) I put my eye to the _____ to see what was under the microscope.
   (b) For many years, Gloria Steinem was a _____ in the women's movement.
   (c) The rescuers enjoyed a brief _____ before sinking back into obscurity.

17C Synonyms, Antonyms, Analogies

Each group of four words below contains two words that are either synonyms or antonyms. Circle these two words; then circle the S if they are synonyms, the A if they are antonyms.

1. BEDIZEN   ABNEGATE
   EMBELLISH   EXTIRPATE   S   A

2. HABITUE   SETTING
   CYNOSURE   MILIEU   S   A

3. DECREE   DEVOLVE
   ABNEGATE   ASSUME   S   A

4. CELERITY   CYNOSURE
   SWIFTNESS   REPARTEE   S   A

5. STAID   INSOUCIANT
   FLAMBOYANT   SYMBIOTIC   S   A

Complete the analogies by selecting the pair of words whose relationship most resembles the relationship of the pair in capital letters. Circle the letter in front of the pair you choose.

6. LISSOME : ELOQUENT ::
   (a) sight : sound   (c) dance : drama
   (b) eye : ear   (d) movement : speech

7. COLLOQUY : BADINAGE ::
   (a) obdurate : flexible   (c) slovenly : debonair
   (b) earnest : jocose   (d) egregious : trifling

8. TYRO : EXPERIENCE ::
   (a) savant : knowledge   (c) indigent : poverty
   (b) demagogue : influence   (d) dilettante : confidence

9. ITINERARY : JOURNEY ::
   (a) score : symphony   (c) panorama : scenery
   (b) exhibit : museum   (d) prescription : medicine

10. OBSTREPEROUS : OUTSPOKEN ::
    (a) vociferous : vehement   (c) fastidious : squeamish
    (b) insouciant : circumspect   (d) solicitous : attentive

17D Images of Words

Circle the letter of each sentence that suggests the numbered boldface vocabulary word. In each group, you may circle more than one letter or none at all.

1. **itinerary**
(a) From Rome, we go to Paris, and then on to Amsterdam.
(b) Geneva's account of her two-thousand-mile journey up the Amazon was published in May.
(c) We had to memorize the names and dates of all of the presidents.

2. ancillary
(a) These are less important matters, so we can deal with them later.
(b) The physical sciences were once viewed as minor branches of philosophy.
(c) The city's needs are considered only after demands of the state are met.

3. tyro
(a) Having had no acting experience, I signed up for the beginners' class.
(b) The cartoon pictured a little dictator.
(c) Because the car was brand new, we were told not to drive it over 55 mph for the first one thousand miles.

4. staid
(a) Mr. Adams wore his habitual dark suit and white shirt to every function he attended.
(b) The opinions offered by Ms. Miniuks were always predictable.
(c) The elders of the family, wearing serious expressions, sat on benches near the wall while the children played on the large lawn.

5. obstreperous
(a) Fallen power lines across the highway made it impossible for us to go on.
(b) Such a sore throat probably needs an anitbiotic.
(c) Our yacht lost time because the wind was against us on the return leg.

6. cynosure
(a) I was embarrassed to see that everyone in the room was staring at me.
(b) Amalia's only responsibility was to be present in the gallery during the day.
(c) In the early 1920s, Rudolph Valentino was Hollywood's greatest star.

7. perquisite
(a) Before they fall, the maple leaves turn to shades of red and gold.
(b) A large sign warned sightseers not to get too close to the edge of the rocks along the coast.
(c) At the end of last shift, the workers get to take home whatever bagels have not been sold.

8. badinage
(a) My remarks were light-hearted and shouldn't be taken seriously.
(b) As we waited for the boat, the wind picked up and we worried about the trip back to the mainland.
(c) The clucking of the hens seemed to come as a reply to the cackling of the geese.

9. symbiosis
(a) Tiffany knows that getting the answers from her friend will not increase her learning.
(b) The crocodile bird, standing astride the crocodile, rids the creature of its parasites.
(c) Throughout nature one can observe many mutually beneficial relationships.

10. **paragon**

(a) In Greek mythology, Helen of Troy was regarded as the supreme example of female beauty.

(b) His sense of superiority prevents him from taking any criticism seriously.

(c) The Washington D.C. metro is the best I've ever ridden.

17E Narrative

Read the narrative below; then complete the exercise that follows it.

ANOTHER COMEBACK KID

In a bit of **badinage** with the press after the New Hampshire primary in February 1992, Bill Clinton declared himself the "Comeback Kid" and wore the title for the rest of the decade. In December 1999, *Sports Illustrated* echoed the familiar epithet and named tennis star Jennifer Capriati "Comeback Player of the Year." To understand what she came back from, we must peek into the pressure-cooker world of professional tennis.

Some time in the past, tennis was a **staid** affair, played purely for the love of it. Although tennis professionals could make a reasonable income teaching club members how to improve their serve or backhand, no one got rich from the game. One of the few **perquisites** of being a champion was the right to sell the use of one's name for a modest sum to a racket manufacturer.

The game changed dramatically in the 1970s when tennis came together with television and big business in a **symbiotic** relationship that generated vast amounts of money and made tennis itself big business. Television viewers were interested in star performers, and an industry arose to supply them. All aspects of the game came under the control of a few large companies. They ran the tennis schools that turned talented **tyros** into world-class superstars. They managed the players' careers and negotiated lucrative contracts with corporate sponsors: soon players' headbands, shirts, shorts, socks, and shoes were **bedizened** with patches advertising a variety of products. These management companies even organized the major tournaments and controlled their television coverage.

In 1990 the reigning queen of tennis, Chris Evert, retired after a twenty-year career, and a newcomer named Jennifer Capriati suddenly became the **cynosure** of fans, television executives, corporate sponsors, and the media. Capriati had dominated the junior tennis circuit the year before, and in March 1990, she turned professional and easily won her first tournament. With her winning smile, **lissome** physique, and relaxed manner, she was Evert's obvious successor. Her father signed her up with the top-rated International Management Group (IMG) because she was too young to sign contracts herself. She was still only thirteen.

That year, Capriati reached the semifinals of the French Open, becoming the youngest player ever to do so. The following year, she defeated the legendary Martina Navratilova to reach the Wimbledon semifinals and did equally well in the United States Open. Her total income for 1991 was just over five million dollars, making her the twenty-sixth highest-paid athlete in the world. Her crowded **itinerary** took her all over the globe, leaving her little time for anything but tennis and **ancillary** activities like giving press interviews and making herself available to sponsors. She appeared to thrive on the attention and enjoyed joking with reporters, telling them in Paris, for example, that Notre Dame was a football team. But beneath the surface poise, pressures were building that those closest to her either would not or could not see.

There was, first of all, the pressure to win. Chris Evert, after all, had won 157 singles championships in her career. There was also the pressure to conduct herself at all times as a **paragon** of virtue in order not to offend sponsors. In 1992, Capriati began to show signs of strain. She quarreled publicly with her father, whose involvement in her career was total. The perfect daughter was becoming an **obstreperous** teenager, and her game suffered. Despite winning a gold medal in the 1992 Olympics, her playing continued to deteriorate. In 1993 she was eliminated in the opening round of the United States Open. At the "ripe old age" of seventeen, Capriati became a has-been. Losing both matches and interest in the game, she **abnegated** her hopes of becoming tennis's reigning queen and slipped into the teenage drug culture. Here was a **milieu** where tennis was not even talked about. Her corporate sponsors abandoned her with the same **celerity** with which, four years earlier, they had signed her up.

Capriati's lost years were 1994 and 1995. Then, in 1996, after rehabilitation, she attempted to get back into the game. She failed to make the Olympic team that year, but in November she beat tennis legend Monica Seles in a Chicago tournament, and then lost in the final. Winning some matches and losing others, she persevered, ignoring setbacks like the injured ankle that sidelined her through much of 1997. It was not until May 1999 that she won a major tournament, her first in six years. Then in January 2000, she celebrated her *Sports Illustrated* Award by winning the Millennium cup in Hong Kong and reaching the semifinals of the Australian Open. Asked to explain her astonishing success, the "Comeback Kid," now twenty-three, replied simply, "I'm not going to put any pressure on myself."

Answer each of the following questions in a sentence. Whenever a vocabulary word does not appear in the question, try to use one (or a form of one) in your answer. In a few cases, both question and answer may contain vocabulary words.

1. Would it be accurate now to describe Jennifer Capriati as a **paragon**? Explain your answer.

2. In what way could the **symbiotic** relationship between television, big business, and tennis lessen the possibilities for those who would like a career in tennis?

   _____

3. What physical and mental qualities would tennis schools look for in a **tyro**?

   _____

4. How would you describe the **milieu** of professional tennis?

   _____

5. Why was tennis bound to change when matches began to be televised?

   _____

6. Why do stars often resemble walking billboards?

   _____

7. What details in the narrative suggest that, as Capriati reached her late teens, conversations between her and her father were not filled with **badinage**?

   _____

8. How did the **perquisites** for tennis professionals change once tennis became big business?

   _____

9. What is your opinion of the management company's treatment of Jennifer Capriati?

   _____

10. What do you think of thirteen-year-old children becoming professional athletes? Explain your answer.

   _____

WORDLY WISE

The North Star can be found at the end of the handle of the Big Dipper, the cluster of seven stars familiar to observers of the night sky in the Northern Hemisphere. The ancient Greeks thought these seven stars looked like a dog, with the North Star forming the tip of its tail. The Greeks called the North Star *kunosoura,* from *kun,* "dog," and *oura,* "tail," and since ancient times the North Star has been considered worthy of attention because it indicates true north. From *kunosoura* comes our word **cynosure,** meaning "something that is the center of attention."

Informally called a *perk,* meaning "a fringe benefit," a **perquisite** is a payment or a profit that an employer gives an employee in addition to wages. The term comes from Middle English, *perquisites,* meaning "property acquired other than by inheritance," and from the Latin *per-,* "for," and *quaerere,* "to seek."

Lesson 18

Word List
Study the words below; then do the exercise for the lesson.

abortive
ə bôr´ tiv

adj. Failing in purpose; unsuccessful.
[After several *abortive* attempts to lower the undercarriage, the pilot was forced to make a crash landing.]

arrogate
ar´ ə gāt

v. To lay claim to without possessing the right to do so.
[The writer Kurt Vonnegut warns of a government *arrogating* to itself rights that belong to the people.]

cadaver
kə da´ vər

n. A dead animal or human body.
[Medical students dissect *cadavers* as part of their training.]
cadaverous *adj.*

cerebral
sə rē´ brəl

adj. **1.** Relating to the brain or intellect.
[A person is declared brain-dead when *cerebral* activity ceases.]
2. Appealing to the intellect, as opposed to the emotions.
[When savants of science meet for a discussion, the colloquy is predictably *cerebral*.]

coma
kō´ mə

n. A state of profound unconsciousness caused by disease or injury.
[The victim was in a *coma* for seven days after being struck on the head.]
comatose *adj.*

consanguinity
kän san gwi´ nə tē

n. A relationship derived from a common ancestor.
[A genealogy shows the degrees of *consanguinity* within a family.]
consanguineous *adj.*

ghoul
gōōl

n. A gruesome and revolting creature.
[The horror movie about *ghouls* coming out of graveyards at midnight was risible rather than terrifying.]
ghoulish *adj.*

infringe
in frinj´

v. **1.** To violate.
[Publishing material without the author's consent *infringes* international copyright law.]
2. (used with *on* or *upon*) To exceed the limits of; to encroach upon.
[By taking an extra ten minutes to finish their set, the players *infringed* upon our court time.]

lassitude
la´ sə tōōd

n. A feeling of weariness; listlessness.
[*Lassitude* usually accompanies a fever and is a sign that a person's body needs rest.]

nadir
nā´ dir

n. The lowest point.
[Toy sales reach their *nadir* in January and do not usually pick up again until after Thanksgiving.]

nuptials
nəp´ shəlz

n. A wedding ceremony.
[Annie and Stephen are planning an August wedding and will hold the *nuptials* on the beach.]
nuptial *adj.* Of or relating to a wedding.

onus ō´ nəs	*n.* Something that must be borne; a burden. [In a criminal case, the *onus* of proof rests with the prosecution.]
protocol prō´ tə kôl	*n.* **1.** A correct code of conduct; etiquette. [Royal *protocol* requires that no one leaves before Her Majesty is ready to depart.] **2.** A standard procedure for a medical treatment or a scientific experiment. [The *protocol* for the pharmaceutical research required a double-blind test.]
refractory ri frak´ tə rē	*adj.* **1.** Failing to yield to treatment. [The *refractory* nature of the disease indicates that the virus is resistant to antibiotics.] **2.** Hard to manage; unruly. [The leaders became alarmed when the concerned group turned into a *refractory* crowd.]
sanguine san´ gwən	*adj.* **1.** Of a healthy red color. [Her *sanguine* complexion was the result of a brisk jog around the park.] **2.** Cheerful and optimistic. [Her *sanguine* personality was a welcome addition to the gloomy atmosphere at the meeting.]

18A Understanding Meanings

Read the sentences in each group below. If a sentence correctly uses the word in boldface, write C on the line of the corresponding number below the group. If a sentence is incorrect, rewrite it so that the vocabulary word in boldface is used correctly.

■ 1. **Lassitude** is a lack of interest in doing things due to diminished energy.
2. A **refractory** case is one that is unresponsive.
3. A **ghoulish** subject is one that is germane.
4. A **cerebral** function is one that is related to the brain.
5. A **coma** is a mark of punctuation, used to indicate a pause.

1. _____

2. _____

3. _____

4. _____

5. _____

■ 6. To **infringe** an agreement is to fail to comply with its terms.
7. A **consanguineous** relationship is one that is cool and distant.
8. An **onus** is paying the restaurant bill for several friends.

9. A **nuptial** planner is one who advises on real estate.
10. A **sanguine** person is one who is not pessimistic.

6. _____

7. _____

8. _____

9. _____

10. _____

■ 11. A **cadaver** is a quibble or petty objection.
12. A **protocol** is an established method for treating a medical condition.
13. A **nadir** is a provincial governor in India.
14. An **abortive** effort is one that does not bring results.
15. To **arrogate** something is to put an end to it.

11. _____

12. _____

13. _____

14. _____

15. _____

18B Using Words

If the word (or a form of the word) in boldface fits in a sentence in the group below it, write the word in the blank space. If the word does not fit, leave the space empty.

1. **sanguine**
   (a) Henry led his armies into many _____ battles.
   (b) Despite numerous setbacks, we are still _____ about the eventual outcome.
   (c) His _____ appearance was evidence of a healthy outdoor life.

2. **infringe**
   (a) One of my colleagues _____ every day on my assigned parking space.
   (b) Several costumes in the museum exhibit have _____ along the hem.
   (c) To cut down a neighbor's tree clearly _____ upon his property rights.

3. **ghoul**
   (a) Behind the terrifying mask of this _____ is a six-year-old trick-or-treater.
   (b) Abisho kicked the soccer ball hard into the _____ and scored a point for his team.
   (c) There is something _____ about gathering to stare at a bad auto accident.

4. **abortive**

    (a) Our efforts to raise the sunken vessel proved _____ , but we will try again.

    (b) After many students made mistakes on the test, my Latin teacher said she would explain again the use of the _____ case.

    (c) We thanked her profusely for all the _____ help she gave us.

5. **protocol**

    (a) Whose responsibility is it to see that the correct medical _____ is followed?

    (b) According to military _____ , rank has its privileges.

    (c) The _____ I took for my bronchitis stopped my coughing.

6. **cadaverous**

    (a) I like rock climbing, but I keep away from _____ places.

    (b) The teenagers were in a _____ mood as they went looking for fun.

    (c) White makeup and heavy black lines gave the actors a _____ look.

7. **onus**

    (a) The recipe for potato-leek soup calls for including some _____ .

    (b) The donkey carried a heavy _____ .

    (c) Leaving a twelve-year-old in charge places a heavy _____ on that child.

8. **cerebral**

    (a) Kim is the _____ type who doesn't have much patience for gothic romances.

    (b) The brain consists of left and right _____ hemispheres.

    (c) The accident was very _____ with the rescue workers needing to use the jaws of life to free the driver from the car.

18C Synonyms, Antonyms, Analogies

Each group of four words below contains two words that are either synonyms or antonyms. Circle these two words; then circle the S if they are synonyms, the A if they are antonyms.

1. ARROGATE   INFRINGE
     RELINQUISH   REPINE   S   A

2. CEREBRAL   SUCCESSFUL
     ANCILLARY   ABORTIVE   S   A

3. CORPSE   CADAVER
    GHOUL   WRAITH   S   A

4. CONSCIOUS   CEREBRAL
    COMATOSE   FATALISTIC   S   A

5. INFRINGE   TRESPASS
    REMOVE   DEVOLVE   S   A

Complete the analogies by selecting the pair of words whose relationship most resembles the relationship of the pair in capital letters. Circle the letter in front of the pair you choose.

6. SANGUINE : COMPLEXION ::
    (a) vernal : spring   (c) azure : sky
    (b) sartorial : clothing   (d) jocose : manner

7. NUPTIAL : MARRIAGE ::
    (a) insolvent : business   (c) amorphous : shape
    (b) infernal : hell   (d) brackish : liquid

8. LASSITUDE : VIGOR ::
    (a) acumen : shrewdness   (c) celerity : haste
    (b) chicanery : rectitude   (d) élan : enthusiasm

9. NADIR : DEBACLE ::
    (a) climax : culmination   (c) zenith : triumph
    (b) tremor : schism   (d) valley : mountain

10. REFRACTORY : DISCIPLINE ::
    (a) equivocal : decision   (c) unethical : censure
    (b) infallible : foible   (d) risible : laughter

18D Images of Words

Circle the letter of each sentence that suggests the numbered boldface vocabulary word. In each group, you may circle more than one letter or none at all.

1. **consanguinity**
(a) Sybil gets along really well with her new college roommate.
(b) I'm related to my cousin Mara on my mother's side.
(c) A parent's artistic talents may be passed on genetically to her or his children.

2. refractory

(a) As often as we cut the dandelions, they sprang back in full yellow bloom.

(b) The X-ray showed a hairline crack in the bone.

(c) We returned the defective tires to the plant where they were made.

3. comatose

(a) Jill was in such a deep sleep that she didn't hear the alarm go off.

(b) The car wouldn't start because the battery was dead.

(c) The patient is breathing but fails to respond to any stimulus.

4. arrogate

(a) Pride is a good thing; excessive pride is another thing.

(b) Cobb pushed aside his partners and took over the running of the small store.

(c) Trujillo took control of all political and economic activity in the Dominican Republic.

5. nadir

(a) The next full moon will be on the thirteenth of February.

(b) The team's worst season was 1988 when they lost all twenty-eight games.

(c) Our situation was so bad that we felt it couldn't possibly get worse.

6. ghoulish

(a) The story describes the grave robbers' activities in graphic detail.

(b) I was shocked when Dan suggested a visit to the city morgue might be fun.

(c) Some people take a delight in other people's misfortunes.

7. cadaver

(a) The detective admitted that an examination of the dead person showed no signs of foul play.

(b) In her will, she has donated her body to science.

(c) A trip to the intensive care unit after an accident might have a sobering effect on convicted drunk drivers.

8. nuptials

(a) Elise says she likes her job but isn't wedded to it.

(b) The couple have written their own wedding vows.

(c) You can be a believer in certain principles without being wedded to them.

9. lassitude

(a) The absence of strict rules enables students to develop their own code of morality.

(b) Those who suffer from chronic fatigue syndrome feel drained of energy.

(c) The extreme tropical heat made walking across the room an effort.

10. cerebral

(a) The blank look on her face suggested that she had not understood my question.

(b) I reminded Michel to wear a hat in the sun to protect his scalp.

(c) Bringing flowers was such a thoughtful gesture.

18E Narrative

Read the narrative below; then complete the exercise that follows.

A FAMILY AFFAIR

The first successful human kidney transplant operations were carried out in the 1950s; then in 1967, Dr. Christiaan Barnard, a South African surgeon, startled the world by performing the first human heart transplant. But despite the headlines, organ transplants then were rare and generally unsuccessful. The most **refractory** problem, rejection by the recipient's immune system, eventually yielded to powerful new drugs. Today successful organ transplants are common, with more than twenty thousand performed each year in the United States.

Liver tissue, bone marrow, even a kidney, can be removed with little risk to the donor, while lungs, hearts, and other vital organs can be harvested only from someone who has recently died, with a strict **protocol** governing these procedures. The organs must be from a person in whom **cerebral** activity has ceased and whose heart and lungs are being maintained by artificial means. Such a person is considered brain-dead; when life-support systems are withdrawn, the **comatose** patient dies immediately.

The best candidates for the harvesting of tissue and organs are the young and healthy. This usually means that donors have died tragically in an accident. The **onus** of giving permission then falls on the next of kin. Approaching grieving relatives at such a time seems almost **ghoulish**. However, consent is needed quickly if the organs are to be saved. The heart, lungs, kidneys, liver, eye corneas, bone, and skin can all be removed from a **cadaver** and given to people desperately in need, some of whom have been waiting for transplants for years. At the start of the new millennium, over sixty thousand Americans were waiting for organ tissue donations, and four thousand a year were dying for lack of one.

Some European countries have laws of "implied consent" under which the state has the right to remove organs from anyone who has died unless that person had specified otherwise beforehand. While almost nine out of ten Americans favor the harvesting of organs, most believe that the state should not **arrogate** to itself the right to decide the issue. Instead, a voluntary system is preferred, even though it is much less proficient at locating donors.

Just such a problem, finding a suitable donor, confronted the parents of Anissa Ayala in 1988 when their daughter began to suffer from unexplained fevers and feelings of **lassitude**. Anissa, not yet sixteen, was a typical, happy-go-lucky California teenager with a boyfriend she intended to marry. A visit to her doctor revealed terrifying news: Anissa was suffering from a form of cancer called myelogenous leukemia. She was given no more than a few years to live. The only thing that might save her was a bone marrow transplant. **Consanguinity** between donor and patient offers the best chance of a match, but neither Anissa's older brother nor her parents proved suitable. A highly publicized, nationwide search for a suitable donor proved **abortive**. The Ayala family's hopes, not too high to begin with, were at their **nadir** when the attempt was abandoned after two years.

In their desperation, Anissa's parents made one last desperate attempt to save her life. Her mother decided to have another child in the hope that it would prove the elusive match to save Anissa's life. Her doctors were far from **sanguine** about the outcome; when the various possibilities were calculated, the chance of success was believed to be one in sixteen. And the Ayala's decisions raised important ethical questions. Was it acceptable to have a child in order to harvest its bone marrow? And if this were done, would it **infringe** on the child's rights since it would be too young to give its consent?

The Ayalas went ahead anyway, and a baby girl, whom they named Marissa, was born in 1990. When Marissa was fourteen months old, some bone marrow was removed from her and given to Anissa. The operation was a success. The Ayalas had beaten the odds. One year later, Anissa married her boyfriend. Attending the **nuptials** as a flower girl was two-year-old Marissa, the little girl who had given her sister a new life.

Answer each of the following questions in a sentence. Whenever a vocabulary word does not appear in the question, try to use one (or a form of one) in your answer. In a few cases, both question and answer may contain vocabulary words.

1. Why might Anissa have been accused of laziness at the onset of her disease?

     _____

2. Why was the **onus** to become donors placed first on Anissa's parents and older brother?

     _____

3. At what point was the Ayala family least **sanguine** about Anissa's survival?

     _____

4. How do we know that Alissa's dream of marrying her boyfriend came true?

     _____

5. Why were early organ transplants frequently **abortive**?

     _____

6. What are some factors that contribute to the shortage of vital organs such as hearts and lungs?

    _____

7. How are the rights of **comatose** patients protected?

    _____

8. What is the intended effect of "implied consent" laws?

    _____

9. Do you think laws of "implied consent" **infringe** on an individual's freedom? Explain your answer.

    _____

WORDLY WISE

Abrogate (Lesson 8) and **arrogate** are both derived from the Latin *rogare*, "to ask," but they have quite different meanings. *Abrogate* uses the Latin *ab*, meaning "away"; to abrogate something is to do away with it. To **arrogate** something is to claim it as one's own without having the right to do so.

The celestial sphere is an imaginary one of infinite extent, on which all heavenly bodies appear to be located. The earth is at the center of this celestial sphere. The zenith is the point on the celestial sphere that is directly above the observer. The point on the celestial sphere diametrically opposite the zenith is the **nadir**. *Zenith* has come to mean "the highest point" while **nadir** means just the opposite.

Sanguinary (Lesson 16) means "marked by the shedding of blood" and is not to be confused with **sanguine**, which means "cheerful." Both words are derived from the Latin *sanguis*, "blood." The connection between *blood* and **sanguine** derives from a belief, held by physicians of the ancient and medieval worlds, that the body was governed by four fluids called humors, from the Latin word for *fluid*. These humors were *cholericus* (yellow bile), *melancholicus* (black bile), *phlegmaticus* (phlegm), and *sanguineus* (blood). Depending on which was dominant, a person could be choleric (angry), melancholy (sad), phlegmatic (easygoing), or **sanguine** (cheerful). An imbalance of these four humors made a person ill-humored; when they were in balance, a person was in good humor, able to laugh or take a joke.

Lesson 19

Word List

Study the definitions of the words below; then do the exercises for the lesson.

appellation
a pə lā´ shən

n. A name other than a legal name that is descriptive of a person or thing.
[In the early nineteenth century, President Andrew Jackson's toughness earned him the *appellation* "Old Hickory."]

conjugal
kän´ ji gəl

adj. Of or related to the married state or married persons.
[The engaged couple looked forward to a life of *conjugal* partnership after the nuptials.]

didactic
dī dak´ tik

adj. **1.** Concerned with teaching or instruction.
[Aesop's fables are *didactic* but never boring.]
2. Too inclined to teach or moralize.
[The critic wrote that the playwright should have eschewed her *didactic* tendencies and concentrated on entertaining the audience.]

efflorescence
e flə re´ səns

n. The process of reaching a peak of development or of coming into flower.
[The *efflorescence* of baroque music is to be found in the operas of Monteverdi.]
efflorescent *adj.* Having the quality of efflorescence.

effulgence
i fôl´ jəns

n. Radiance; splendor; brilliance.
[To capture on canvas the *effulgence* of the eastern sky at sunrise is a challenge to any painter.]
effulgent *adj.*

exegesis
ek sə je´ səs

n. A critical explanation or interpretation.
[Without the accompanying *exegesis*, it is easy to misconstrue the meaning of this text.]

genre
zhän´ rə

n. A kind, sort, or category, often used to classify an artistic composition.
[Nobel Prize winner Nadine Gordimer wrote in the *genre* of the short story as well as that of the novel.]

limn
lim

v. **1.** To draw or paint.
[The artist used charcoal to *limn* the outline of the distant mountain peak.]
2. To describe or depict.
[The scene in the apothecary's shop is *limned* so well that the reader can almost smell the aromatic herbs.]

miscreant
mis´ krē ənt

n. A villain or criminal.
[This psychologist believes that places of poverty can produce *miscreants*.]

mordant
môr´ dənt

adj. Sharp and penetrating in manner or style; trenchant.
[Writer Dorothy Parker's *mordant* wit stemmed in large measure from her own desperate unhappiness.]

mores
môr´ āz

n. pl. **1.** The accepted customs, attitudes, or manners of a group.
[My friend from Iran helped me understand the *mores* of Muslim society.]
2. Morally binding ways of a particular group.
[The professor of sociology emphasized that a culture without *mores* would lack cohesion.]

nemesis neʹ mə səs	*n.* **1.** A formidable, usually victorious, rival. [Her arrogance may be cracked when she meets her *nemesis* on the tennis court.] **2.** One who inflicts punishment or retribution. [Captain Ahab's *nemesis* was Moby Dick, the great white whale.]
peccadillo pe kə diʹ lō	*n.* A minor fault; a petty offense. [Each of the author's youthful *peccadilloes* is sedulously recorded in this interminable memoir.]
prolix prō liksʹ	*adj.* Given to using excessive words; long and drawn out. [An hour into his speech, the *prolix* candidate was just warming up.] **prolixity** *n.* Wordiness.
taciturn taʹ sə tərn	*adj.* Reluctant to talk; habitually silent. [When greeted with a warm hello and a touch on the arm, the *taciturn* young woman simply smiled and walked on.] **taciturnity** *n.* The quality of speaking very infrequently.

19A Understanding Meanings

Read the sentences in each group below. If a sentence correctly uses the word in boldface, write C on the line of the corresponding number below the group. If a sentence is incorrect, rewrite it so that the vocabulary word in boldface is used correctly.

■ 1. A **conjugal** visit is one that occurs between people who are married.
    2. An **effulgent** stream is one that is flowing out from a source.
    3. A **peccadillo** is a slight mistake.
    4. To **limn** a scene is to sketch it.
    5. **Taciturnity** is an unwillingness to yield.

1. _____

2. _____

3. _____

4. _____

5. _____

■ 6. An **exegesis** is a carcinogen.
    7. A **didactic** approach is one that emphasizes learning.
    8. **Mores** are foibles.
    9. **Efflorescence** is the blossoming or culmination of a process.
    10. A **miscreant** is a thespian.

6. _____

7. _____

8. _____

9. _____

10. _____

■ 11. **Prolixity** is verbosity.
12. An **appellation** is a dissertation.
13. A **nemesis** is a trick or method used to aid memory.
14. A **genre** is a specific type of literary or musical category.
15. A **mordant** essay is one dealing with death or dying.

11. _____

12. _____

13. _____

14. _____

15. _____

19B Using Words

If the word (or a form of the word) in boldface fits in a sentence in the group below it, write the word in the blank space. If the word does not fit, leave the space empty.

1. **efflorescence**
   (a) The Athens of fifth century B.C. saw an amazing _____ of the arts.
   (b) After their vernal display, the gardens reach a second _____ in the fall.
   (c) The water flows into an _____ that carries it away in buried pipes.

2. **prolix**
   (a) The cherries were so _____ that year that we picked them by the bushel.
   (b) It was my job to reduce the more _____ reports to a single page or less.
   (c) The author uses such _____ words that I don't understand half of them.

3. **limn**
   (a) The dealer said I could _____ a few notes to hear how the violin sounded.
   (b) He likes to _____ the outlines of a scene in pencil before applying oil paint.
   (c) Elizabeth Gaskell could _____ an unforgettable character by using several well-chosen details.

4. **exegesis**
   (a) The author should provide an _____ of the more difficult passages.
   (b) Rosario could offer no _____ for her unexpected absence from the house.
   (c) A detailed _____ in the form of footnotes accompanies the text.

5. **mores**
   (a) Victorian middle class _____ provide the background to Trollope's novels.
   (b) A knowledge of Arab _____ is helpful to those doing business in Kuwait.
   (c) The Nigerian ambassador has a superb collection of African _____ .

6. **miscreant**
   (a) Driving without a license is considered a serious traffic _____ .
   (b) The _____ was a faulty exhaust fan that trapped stale air inside the classroom.
   (c) Should a _____ be rewarded with a lucrative book deal that recounts his story?

7. **nemesis**
   (a) J. Edgar Hoover enjoyed seeing himself portrayed as the criminals' _____ .
   (b) The unlucky revelers were caught in a _____ of their own making.
   (c) Moriarty found himself face to face with his old _____ , Sherlock Holmes.

8. **genre**
   (a) Twelve-tone music was a _____ with which I happened to be familiar.
   (b) We usually buy a Chevrolet, but this year we're trying a different _____ .
   (c) Portraiture was not the only _____ in which Mary Cassatt excelled.

19C Synonyms, Antonyms, Analogies

Each group of four words below contains two words that are either synonyms or antonyms. Circle these two words; then circle the S if they are synonyms, the A if they are antonyms.

1. CEREBRAL   DIM
   EFFULGENT   VERNAL   S   A

2. PROLIXITY   DECLINE
   EFFLORESCENCE   EXEGESIS   S   A

3. CAUSTIC   MORDANT

    CONJUGAL   EVASIVE   S   A

4. PARAGON   EXEGESIS

    PARTICIPANT   MISCREANT   S   A

5. TACITURN   UNEASY

    PROLIX   REFRACTORY   S   A

Complete the analogies by selecting the pair of words whose relationship most resembles the relationship of the pair in capital letters. Circle the letter in front of the pair you choose.

6. CONJUGAL : MARRIAGE ::
   - (a) insipid : taste
   - (b) staccato : sound
   - (c) juvenile : childhood
   - (d) svelte : shape

7. PECCADILLO : CRIME ::
   - (a) fib : lie
   - (b) thespian : actor
   - (c) encomium : calumny
   - (d) truth : verisimilitude

8. DIDACTIC : TEACH ::
   - (a) iconoclastic : conform
   - (b) sycophantic : flatter
   - (c) invidious : compare
   - (d) obdurate : yield

9. GENRE : MUSIC ::
   - (a) domain : territory
   - (b) sibling : family
   - (c) land : field
   - (d) verisimilitude : truth

10. SOCIETY : MORES ::
    - (a) humankind : festivals
    - (b) miscreant : schemes
    - (c) peccadilloes : flaws
    - (d) tribe : customs

19D Images of Words

Circle the letter of each sentence that suggests the numbered boldface vocabulary word. In each group, you may circle more than one letter or none at all.

1. **conjugal**
   - (a) Some high schools have courses that include a discussion about the seriousness of marriage.
   - (b) My Latin course requires that I understand the grammar of verbs.
   - (c) Some prisoners are allowed monthly overnight visits from their wives.

2. effulgence

(a) The sunlight beamed off the Tiffany glass lampshade.

(b) Sonia Delauney made use of primary colors in her abstract paintings.

(c) The flickering light from the lantern cast grotesque shadows as we entered the barn.

3. peccadillo

(a) After less than a mile, Joanne was complaining of sore feet and aching muscles.

(b) Thieves got away with half a million dollars in yesterday's bank robbery.

(c) The bumper sticker on the car read "Hugs not Drugs."

4. mordant

(a) She absolutely loves to read murder mysteries.

(b) The drowning man was near death when the lifeguard got to him.

(c) The audience was unprepared for the comedian's biting humor.

5. taciturnity

(a) The reason for Carla's unaccustomed silence was that she had fallen asleep.

(b) A question on an essay test requires more than a single sentence answer.

(c) We had vacationed in the small village for several years before the townspeople began to speak to us.

6. appellation

(a) Because he found a wrecked vessel containing rich cargo, the Icelandic explorer Leif Ericson was thereafter called "Lucky Leif."

(b) She challenged me to name one person who would vote for the measure.

(c) It was in such bad shape that "coffin ship" aptly described the boat.

7. exegesis

(a) Moses led the Jews from Egypt into the land of Canaan.

(b) Her essay gives one interpretation of Robert Musil's *The Man without Qualities*.

(c) The swing set comes with a full set of instructions for its assembly.

8. mores

(a) After living in Brooklyn, she needs time to adjust to life in the small Iowa town.

(b) Anthropologist Margaret Mead learned a great deal about the Samoan people by living among them.

(c) When we camped out, I loved eating those cookies made with marshmallows, graham crackers, and chocolate.

9. limn

(a) His journal entry for the day read, "Nothing happened."

(b) I said you can draw your own conclusions as to the likely result.

(c) She took a stick and drew an outline in the sand for a game of hopscotch.

10. **didactic**

(a) Her ideas are often good, but she expresses them too forcefully.

(b) "Advice. Advice. Advice. I'm tired of it!"

(c) These games are designed to develop a child's verbal abilities.

19E Narrative

Read the narrative below; then complete the exercise that follows it.

TWO-DIMENSIONAL ENTERTAINMENT

A number of significant events occurred in 1895. Cuba rebelled against Spanish rule, paving the way for the Spanish-American War three years later. Marconi invented wireless telegraphy, transforming global communication. The first movies were shown in a Paris theater. And the American comic strip was born. Its name was "Hogan's Alley." Appearing in the *New York Sunday World*, it dealt with life in the squalid tenements of New York's Lower East Side. This first real comic strip illustrated the **peccadilloes** of a jug-eared, bald-headed street kid who lived with a pet goat and parrot. He and his friends perpetrated pranks on unsuspecting adults; smoked and drank on occasion, an indication of what some viewed as the permissive **mores** of the period; and engaged in the rough street humor familiar to its big city readers.

When, a year later, the rival *New York Journal* started its color supplement, a major journalistic innovation, it boasted that "the **effulgence** of its eight pages would make the rainbow look like a lead pipe." One of the first things its editor did was lure away from the *World* the illustrator of "Hogan's Alley." He renamed the strip "The Yellow Kid," an **appellation** derived from the color of the principal character's customary attire, a long, dirty nightshirt that reached to his ankles.

In the days before radio and television, comic strips were one of the few sources of entertainment available to anyone with a penny, the cost of a daily newspaper. The significant boost they could give to circulation was not lost on the owners of the newspaper. This was a time when the printed word was paramount, with three-volume novels still popular. It is not surprising, therefore, that the characters in these early comic strips were **prolix**; it was not uncommon for a hundred words or more to be crammed into a single dialog balloon. Their modern counterparts are **taciturn** in comparison, usually getting their point across in a dozen words or fewer.

Sometimes called "the funnies," comic strips often contain far more than laughs. Social satire made its appearance in "Bringing up Father," which revolves around Maggie and Jiggs, a working-class Irish immigrant couple who win the Irish Sweepstakes and move to New York's Fifth Avenue. Their **conjugal** life is punctuated but never seriously threatened by their numerous spats. The strip provided abundant opportunities to poke fun at the foibles of the rich as well as the pretensions of those who found themselves newly rich. A classic of the **genre,** it first appeared in 1913 and was still going strong by the end of the century.

The decade of the 1920s was the golden age of the comic strip. "Gasoline Alley" first appeared in strip form at the very beginning of the decade, although it had appeared in single-frame format two years before. It dealt with life in small town America, particularly as it was affected by that newfangled contraption, the automobile. This cartoon, like "Bringing up Father," continues today, its popularity sustained by another artist who succeeded the strip's creator.

In 1924, the publisher of the *Chicago Tribune* looked at some preliminary sketches for a comic strip about an orphan boy with a curly head of hair and a face **limned** so sparingly that his eyes, (o o), were indistinguishable from letters of the alphabet. He was to be "Little Orphan Otto"; however, many strips starred boys rather than girls, so artist Harold Gray created "Little Orphan Annie" instead. With its story line running for many episodes, "Annie" was almost a novel in comic-book form. It inspired several movies, a radio show, and a successful Broadway musical.

"Popeye," in 1929, became the first superhero of the comics, his amazing strength fueled by cans of spinach. His modest "I yam what I yam an' that's all I yam," became a national catch phrase. The 1920s had just ended when "Dick Tracy" (1931) first appeared. It featured an army of **miscreants,** with names like Prune Face and Flattop, whose heads and faces were drawn to match their names. Action developed as they were pursued by their **nemesis,** the G-man with the jutting jaw and famous two-way wrist radio.

The post-World War II comic strips took on a more **didactic** role, offering social and political commentary. Charles Schultz's "Peanuts," which began in 1950, did so with gentle humor, wisdom, and pathos. Charlie Brown's search for his identity, Snoopy's heroic fantasies, Lucy's world-weary attitude, and Linus's security blanket all struck psychological chords with readers. "Peanuts" even inspired a best-selling book, *The Gospel According to Peanuts,* which provided an **exegesis** of the comic strip's moral and spiritual implications. When Charles Schultz unexpectedly announced his retirement because of ill health in 1999 and died a few weeks later, about 350 million readers mourned his passing and the termination of his strip. It was then the world's most widely read comic, appearing in almost 3,000 newspapers in 60 countries and in 20 languages. Many believe its astonishingly wide appeal resulted from its ability to speak to what is human in us all.

The **mordant** humor of Walt Kelly's "Pogo" cut deeper. In 1971, in a series devoted to showing the destruction to the environment, Kelly coined the phrase, "We have met the enemy, and he is us." It became the official motto of that year's Earth Day. Gary Trudeau's satirical "Doonesbury," which received a Pulitzer Prize in 1975, targets national political figures.

Social historians point to three major contributions by the United States to world culture in the twentieth century, and all three trace their origins back to the 1890s. They are jazz, which has its roots in the African-American work songs and spirituals; the stage musical, which began in the English music halls but reached its **efflorescence** on Broadway in the 1920s; and the most unassuming of the three—the comic strip.

Answer each of the following questions in a sentence. Whenever a vocabulary word does not appear in the question, try to use one (or a form of one) in your answer. In a few cases, both question and answer may contain vocabulary words.

1. When did the comic strip reach its **efflorescence?**

_____

2. Why could the *Journal* boast of the **effulgence** of its supplement?

_____

3. How did the balance between words and pictures in the comic strip change over the years?

_____

4. Why would it be inaccurate to describe the street kid in "Hogan's Alley" as a **miscreant?**

_____

5. Would you describe the marriage of Maggie and Jiggs as a happy one? Explain your answer.

_____

6. How has "Little Orphan Annie" been translated into other **genres?**

_____

7. Explain why "Little Orphan Annie" might have had a different **appellation.**

_____

8. What was distinctive about the way many of the characters in "Dick Tracy" were **limned?**

_____

9. How were the comic strips in the 1950s different from those that had preceded them?

_____

10. How would you describe the phrase, "We have met the enemy, and he is us."?

_____

WORDLY WISE

In Greek mythology, Nemesis was the goddess who pursued and inflicted an appropriate punishment on those who had broken the divine law. The word nemesis has passed unchanged into English, except for the dropping of the capital *n,* and refers to harm or ruin brought about by one's own failings or to the agent that brings about such ruin or harm.

The Latin *tacere,* "to be silent," forms the root of taciturn. Another word sharing this root is *tacit*, "unspoken." A tacit agreement is one that is understood without anything being said.

Lesson 20

Word List

Study the definitions of the words below; then do the exercises for the lesson.

despoil
di spoil´

v. To strip of belongings or worth.
[Unrestricted dumping of toxic chemicals had *despoiled* the area and made it uninhabitable.]
despoliation *n.*

educe
i do͞os´

v. To conclude from given facts; to work out through reasoning.
[From accumulated data, scientists will attempt to *educe* where the hurricane will strike land.]

equable
e´ kwa bəl

adj. **1.** Not varying; steady.
[The Gulf Stream off the Florida coast maintains an *equable* temperature of 80 degrees.]
2. Not easily disturbed; serene.
[Carolina's manner remains *equable* despite the pressures of family, relationships, and corporate life.]

happenstance
ha´ pən stans

n. A circumstance due to chance.
[Just by *happenstance*, we found a gold ring in the sand.]

insular
in´ so͞o lər

adj. **1.** Relating to an island or island people.
[Many residents of Tokyo are cosmopolitan in attitude despite Japan's *insular* position.]
2. Resistant to new or different ideas.
[The Amish are an independent and *insular* people who exist amid a diversified, larger world.]

mayhem
mā´ hem

n. Deliberate and willful infliction of violent injury or destruction.
[In 1987, armored government troops created *mayhem* when they confronted pro-democracy demonstrators in Beijing's Tiananmen Square.]

parlous
pär´ ləs

adj. Fraught with uncertainty, risk, or danger.
[Ireland had been through *parlous* times in the past, most notably the Great Potato Famine of the 1840s.]

pellucid
pə lo͞o´ səd

adj. **1.** Extremely clear; transparent.
[The ocean floor eighty feet below was clearly visible through the *pellucid* waters off the Jamaican coast.]
2. Expressed simply; easily understood.
[The valedictorian's *pellucid* speech made his meaning impossible to misconstrue.]

preclude
pri klo͞od´

v. To make impossible; to prevent.
[His meticulous preparation *precluded* the audience from asking hasty questions.]

propinquity
prə piŋ´ kwə te´

n. A closeness in position.
[The *propinquity* of the twin oak trees in the garden made suspending the hammock a simple task.]

rapacious
rə pā´ shəs

adj. Taking without restraint; greedy or grasping.
[*Rapacious* looting followed the riots.]

schism
siz´ əm

n. A division in a group due to discord.
[A *schism* among Republicans led to the formation of the Bull Moose Party in the 1912 presidential election.]

sublimate
sə´ blə māt

v. To redirect one's impulses or instincts to a more socially acceptable expression.
[Although justifiably angry, she *sublimated* her urge to scream by going out and taking a run.]

talisman
ta´ ləs mən

n. An object believed to have magical powers.
[This engraved stone from the South Pacific is a *talisman*, which is supposed to ward off sickness.]
talismanic *adj.*

terrestrial
tə res´ trē əl

adj. **1.** Relating to the earth or its inhabitants.
[Observers of the strange object in the sky were obdurate in their belief that it was not of *terrestrial* origin.]
2. Of or relating to land, as opposed to water.
[The railroad is a *terrestrial* form of transportation.]

20A Understanding Meanings

Read the sentences in each group below. If a sentence correctly uses the word in boldface, write C on the line of the corresponding number below the group. If a sentence is incorrect, rewrite it so that the vocabulary word in boldface is used correctly.

■ 1. **Propinquity** is the state of being nearby.
2. An **insular** person is insidious.
3. To **educe** something is to dismiss it as being of no importance.
4. A **schism** is a division within a group.
5. A **talisman** is a person who keeps score in an athletic contest.

1. _____
2. _____
3. _____
4. _____
5. _____

■ 6. An **equable** temperament is one that is not easily disturbed.
7. **Mayhem** is uncertainty how to respond or behave.
8. A **parlous** situation is one that is desperate.
9. To **sublimate** a drive is to direct it into acceptable channels.
10. A **terrestrial** means of transportation moves on water.

6. _____

7. _____

8. _____

9. _____

10. _____

■ 11. A **happenstance** is a result of fortune.

12. To **preclude** an event is to preview it.

13. A **rapacious** person is one who talks loudly and continually.

14. To **despoil** an area is to ruin it.

15. A **pellucid** translation is one that is very clear.

11. _____

12. _____

13. _____

14. _____

15. _____

20B Using Words

If the word (or a form of the word) in boldface fits in a sentence in the group below it, write the word in the blank space. If the word does not fit, leave the space empty.

1. **parlous**
   (a) By the early 1930s, the country's economy was in a _____ state.
   (b) I ignored the _____ looks I was getting and continued with my remarks
   (c) Our circumstances on the mountain were looking increasingly _____ .

2. **happenstance**
   (a) It was sheer _____ that brought us together after a ten-year separation.
   (b) Each _____ was recorded in detail in the journal Mellors kept.
   (c) Where the hot-air balloon returned to earth depended on _____ .

3. **educe**
   (a) It is impossible to _____ the answer from the information given.
   (b) We tried to _____ her to stay longer, but her mind was made up.
   (c) From very few clues, Poirot was able to _____ the murderer's identity.

4. **terrestrial**
    (a) The invention of the wheel revolutionized _____ transportation.
    (b) The first _____ creatures appeared about 350 million years ago.
    (c) A _____ telescope is not designed for viewing the moon and planets.

5. **rapacious**
    (a) A _____ property owner can take advantage of desperate renters.
    (b) Ranchers blame _____ coyotes for most of their sheep losses.
    (c) Flying a light plane under the Golden Gate Bridge was a most _____ act.

6. **mayhem**
    (a) If the two small planes had collided, the result would have been _____ .
    (b) Police broke up the gathering just as _____ was about to erupt.
    (c) The ringleaders of the riot were charged with conspiracy to commit _____ .

7. **sublimate**
    (a) The artist sought to _____ his rage at society into powerful works of art.
    (b) We attempted to _____ the various points of view into a single statement.
    (c) Why can't you two _____ your differences and be friends?

8. **preclude**
    (a) My Caribbean vacation does not _____ a European trip later in the year.
    (b) Why did you _____ the Andersons when you sent out the invitations?
    (c) The brevity of my report must _____ a detailed description of the prototype.

20C Synonyms, Antonyms, Analogies

Each group of four words below contains two words that are either synonyms or antonyms. Circle these two words; then circle the S if they are synonyms, the A if they are antonyms.

1. INSULAR	CHANGEABLE		
SYMBIOTIC	EQUABLE	S	A
2. RESTORATION	DESPOLIATION		
PROPINQUITY	LASSITUDE	S	A

3. PRODIGAL   PELLUCID
    POSITIVE   BENEFICENT   S   A

4. SUBLIMATE   ALLOW
    SUBSUME   PRECLUDE   S   A

5. HAPPENSTANCE   MAYHEM
    PROPINQUITY   PROXIMITY   S   A

Complete the analogies by selecting the pair of words whose relationship most resembles the relationship of the pair in capital letters. Circle the letter in front of the pair you choose.

6. TERRESTRIAL : EARTH ::
    (a) vacuous : vacuum   (c) planetary : orbit
    (b) lunar : moon   (d) effulgent : sun

7. INSULAR : ISLAND ::
    (a) hectic : city   (c) miniature : microcosm
    (b) parochial : parish   (d) tropical : equator

8. PELLUCID : CLARITY ::
    (a) taciturn : prolixity   (c) heterogeneous : variety
    (b) amorphous : form   (d) acerbic : sweetness

9. DISCORD : SCHISM ::
    (a) calumny : divorce   (c) altercation : unanimity
    (b) nemesis : retribution   (d) privation : disarray

10. PARLOUS : PERIL ::
    (a) onerous : omen   (c) deceitful : treachery
    (b) ascetic : asperity   (d) amorphous : solidity

20D Images of Words

Circle the letter of each sentence that suggests the numbered boldface vocabulary word. In each group, you may circle more than one letter or none at all.

1. insular

(a) A layer of thick blubber keeps the seals warm in the frigid water.

(b) The expatriates live in one section and so far have not mixed much with the native-born of the country.

(c) The fact that Britain was an island protected it from invasion.

2. despoliation
(a) The meat smelled bad, so rather than risk eating it we disposed of it.
(b) Over-farming turned the fertile plain into a barren dustbowl.
(c) Not a tree was left in the crater of the volcano.

3. pellucid
(a) I like to clear my desk before leaving on Friday afternoon for the weekend.
(b) The translation of this short story from French into English retains the remarkable clarity of the original.
(c) The glass is six inches thick yet so clear that it is practically invisible.

4. talisman
(a) The chairperson began to tally up the votes, hoping the motion she favored would pass.
(b) Sheila really believes that her rabbit's foot brings her good luck.
(c) The word *abracadabra* was once believed to have magical properties.

5. propinquity
(a) The lovers walked arm in arm.
(b) Symmes is a keen golfer and bought a house overlooking the golf course.
(c) In this town, most lawyers' offices are within walking distance of the courthouse.

6. happenstance
(a) The shortstop positioned himself perfectly to catch the fly ball.
(b) My three roommates and I all happen to wear the same size clothes.
(c) We met on a bus in 1971, and we have remained friends ever since.

7. sublimate
(a) There are fewer problems in the cafeteria now that the children go outside to recess after eating.
(b) Ming is determined to stop worrying about things he cannot control.
(c) She gets rid of her frustrations with the government by writing protest songs.

8. schism
(a) The gap between the haves and the have-nots widened during the 1990s.
(b) It took twelve stitches to close the cut in the swimmer's leg.
(c) Some members of the club could not agree with its regulations, so they dropped out and formed a similar organization of their own.

9. mayhem
(a) I couldn't make myself heard because everyone was yelling at once.
(b) The room was so messy that it looked as if a wild wind had blown through an open window.
(c) The coach stopped the hockey game when fists flew and sticks were swung.

10. **equable**

(a) Josh was an ideal traveling companion because nothing seemed to upset him.

(b) The climate of Guyana varies little from one season to the next.

(c) There is no difference between three times six and six times three.

20E Narrative   *Read the narrative below; then complete the exercise that follows it.*

RAPA NUI

During the second half of the twentieth century the world's population has doubled from two-and-a-half billion to five billion. During this period, **rapacious** timber barons have axed great tropical rain forests essential to the planet's health at the rate of thirty acres a minute. At the same time, books like Al Gore's *Earth in the Balance: Ecology and the Human Spirit* and Jonathan Schell's *The Fate of the Earth* warned of the dangers of continued **despoliation** of the planet and the proliferation of nuclear weapons. While contemporary indicators alert us to such dangers, so does history. By studying a place as small and remote as Rapa Nui, in the South Pacific, 2,300 miles west of Chile, we can **educe** the consequences of unchecked carelessness, greed, and aggression.

Archaeological evidence suggests that Rapa Nui was first settled around A.D. 400 by Polynesians forced by the pressures of overpopulation in their native islands to cross many hundreds of miles of open ocean in search of new lands. With no maps or navigational aids to guide them, most expeditions disappeared without a trace, but **happenstance** brought one party of perhaps fifty people to the island they called Rapa Nui, formed by the **propinquity** of three active volcanoes and their lava. Fourteen miles long and seven miles wide, it was a place where trees, mostly palms, grew in abundance in the fertile soil, but where the island's animal life comprised mostly insects, worms, and spiders with no **terrestrial** mammals.

The settlers cleared trees and planted the taros, yams, sweet potatoes, bananas, and sugarcane they had brought. The **pellucid** waters around the island yielded a rich harvest of fish, and the **equable** subtropical climate made for a life of relative ease. As their numbers increased, the inhabitants divided into clans, engaging in a natural, friendly rivalry.

An **insular** society, undisturbed by the outside world for fifty generations, Rapa Nui developed a culture that included the Rongorongo script, the only written language in Oceania; petroglyphs; and giant stone statues, called Moai, that bordered the coastline. These, the island's most spectacular sight, averaging 15 feet in height and weighing many tons, were believed to hold the spirits of the departed. The island's religion, based on ancestor worship, was centered around the Moai that were believed to have **talismanic** powers. Clans gained status by erecting these monoliths. Some might say that the islanders **sublimated** their aggressive impulses in a nonviolent form of competition since the clan with the biggest and greatest number of statues was supposed to be favored by the gods.

By around 1500, the population of Rapa Nui had reached about seven thousand, straining the island's ecosystem. Forests that had once covered the island had been almost entirely cleared, **precluding** the possibility of building large, ocean-going canoes that might have made migration to other islands possible. **Schisms** among the clans grew deeper, and the social order eventually collapsed, giving way to **mayhem**. For the next three hundred years, internecine war raged intermittently on the island. Food became so scarce that researchers believe the islanders may have resorted to cannibalism as a means of survival.

On Easter Sunday, 1722, the crew of a Dutch ship visited the island, ending thirteen centuries of isolation. They called it Easter Island, the name by which it is commonly known today. Fifty years later, a British ship, the Endeavor, came to the island. By then, its people were in a **parlous** state; its population had been reduced to less than seven hundred, with fewer than thirty women. Desecration of the statues occurred when all were toppled from their platforms.

Today, Easter Island is part of Chile and is relatively prosperous; its population of just over two thousand engages mostly in agriculture and fishing. Its airport, built in the early 1950s, was improved in 1970 to handle jet aircraft, giving a boost to tourism, the third leg of its economy. Visitors are enchanted by the great statues and awestruck by their grandeur, but those who know something of Rapa Nui's history understand that the island is more than just a vacation destination. It can be seen as a microcosm of the world at large, a reminder of the threat that population pressures and heedless destruction of the environment pose.

Answer each of the following questions in a sentence. Whenever a vocabulary word does not appear in the question, try to use one (or a form of one) in your answer. In a few cases, both the question and the answer may contain vocabulary words.

1. Why were three separate volcanoes able to form a single island?

_____

2. How do we know that **happenstance** brought its original discoverers to Rapa Nui?

_____

3. What details in the narrative suggest that Rapa Nui could be described as an earthly paradise?

_____

4. What forms of **terrestrial** flora were most abundant on the island?

_____

5. Why could Rapa Nui be fairly described as a quintessentially **insular** society?

_____

6. How did the monoliths help maintain the peace of the community for many years?

_____

7. What do the **putative** claims of cannibalism on the island indicate?

_____

8. What lesson can be **educed** from the history of Rapa Nui?

_____

9. What are some examples you can provide of the **despoliation** of the planet?

_____

WORDLY WISE

Equitable (Lesson 15) and **equable** are both formed from the Latin *equi*, "even," but they have quite different meanings and applications. *Equitable* pertains to even-handedness in sharing. An *equitable* arrangement is one that is fair to all parties involved. *Equable* pertains to evenness in terms of no large fluctuations. An *equable* climate is one without extremes; an *equable* temperament is one without marked changes in mood.

A "portmanteau" word is one formed by merging the sounds and meanings of two separate words into one. (Linguists use the word *conflating* to describe this.) The portmanteau word **happenstance** was created by an unknown writer to mean "a circumstance that happens by chance."

Crossword Puzzle

Solve the crossword puzzle below by studying the clues and filling in the answer boxes. Clues followed by a number are definitions of words in lessons 17 through 20. The number gives the word list from which the answer to the clue is taken.

Clues Across

1. To renounce, as a right or claim (17)
4. Moving or bending easily; supple (17)
9. Capital of Peru
10. Wilful infliction of violent injury (20)
11. Intended to teach or instruct (19)
12. A burden that must be borne (18)
13. A setting in which events occur (17)
14. Sharp and penetrating; trenchant (19)
16. Resistant to new or different ideas (20)
17. A source of deserved harm or ruin (19)
22. Light, playful conversation (17)
23. Failing to yield to treatment (18)
25. Second to; subordinate (17)
28. Sedate; restrained (17)
30. To describe or depict (19)
31. To work out through reasoning (20)
32. Length times width
33. A category of artistic composition (19)

Clues Down

2. To decorate in a gaudy fashion (17)
3. Reluctant to talk; habitually silent (19)
4. Canine movie star
5. Mutually cooperative and beneficial (17)
6. Garden of _____
7. Capital of Austria
8. A feeling of weariness; listlessness (18)
15. Type of automobile tire
16. To exceed the limits of; to encroach (18)
18. The accepted customs of a group (19)
19. A model of perfection (17)
20. Given to excessive wordiness (19)
21. A measure of gasoline performance
24. The lowest point (18)
26. A state of deep unconsciousness (18)
27. Ivy league university
29. Worn around the neck